Come, Lord Jesus

Come, Lord Jesus

TIMELESS HOMILIES FOR ADVENT AND CHRISTMAS

Bishop Robert Barron

WORD on FIRE

Published by Word on Fire, Elk Grove Village, IL 60007

Printed in the United States of America

Cover design, typesetting, and interior art direction by Cassie Bielak

First printing, October 2023

ISBN: 978-1-68578-071-5

Library of Congress Control Number: 2023940920

CONTENTS

The Fourth Week of Advent

Christmas Day

The Christmas Season

THE FIRST WEEK of ADVENT

"Stay awake! For you do not know on
which day your Lord will come."

—MATTHEW 24:42

WE NEED A SAVIOR

Isaiah 63:16b–17, 19b; 64:2–7 (Year B)

You, LORD, are our father,
our redeemer you are named forever.
Why do you let us wander, O LORD, from your ways,
and harden our hearts so that we fear you not?
Return for the sake of your servants,
the tribes of your heritage.
Oh, that you would rend the heavens and come down,
with the mountains quaking before you,
While you wrought awesome deeds we could not hope for,
such as they had not heard of from of old.
No ear has ever heard, no eye ever seen, any God but you
doing such deeds for those who wait for him.
Would that you might meet us doing right,
that we were mindful of you in our ways!
Behold, you are angry, and we are sinful;
all of us have become like unclean people,
all our good deeds are like polluted rags;
We have all withered like leaves,
and our guilt carries us away like the wind.
There is none who calls upon your name,
who rouses himself to cling to you;
For you have hidden your face from us

and have delivered us up to our guilt.
Yet, O LORD, you are our father;
we are the clay and you the potter:
we are all the work of your hands.

And so we begin the Advent season, the time of waiting and watching. Here is the single biggest challenge of this season: really to feel our need for a savior! We tend to domesticate Christ, reducing him to a guru, a teacher, a spiritual guide, a wise philosopher. But that does violence to the Gospel, which presents him not simply as teacher but as Savior. Jesus has rescued us, saved us, done something that we could never, even in principle, do for ourselves. Until we truly feel what it means to be lost and helpless, we will not appreciate who Jesus is and what he means.

It's helpful here to reflect on the meaning of the word *redemption*. *Redimere* means to "buy back" in Latin. It's a term that was used to describe the process of the release of a person who was kidnapped. Someone is held for ransom, and once the ransom is paid, he has been "redeemed." If you are kidnapped, you are held captive; there is not much you can do except wait for someone to save you. "O come, O come, Emmanuel, and ransom captive Israel": let the meaning of that single line from the most famous Advent hymn sink into your heart. Only then will you truly understand the meaning of this season. It's as though we are prisoners: we can't save ourselves, so we wait and we watch.

In many ways, the culture, which steadily teaches the ideology of self-esteem and self-assertion, militates against Christianity at this point, saying, "I'm okay and you're okay" or "Who are you to tell me how to behave?" But this sort of thing—whatever value it might have politically or psychologically—is simply inimical to a biblical Christianity. The biblical view is that we have, through the abuse of our freedom, gotten ourselves into an impossible bind. Sin has compromised us in such a fundamental way that we become, spiritually speaking, dysfunctional.

We are made for love and connection and justice and nonviolence, but at every turn and in every way, we are twisted in the direction of hatred, separation, injustice, and violence. We are, as St. Augustine put it, wandering in the land of dissimilitude and in the grip of the *libido dominandi* (lust for domination). The contemporary philosopher René Girard has reminded us that all of our social arrangements are marked by scapegoating and oppression. If we doubt any of this, I would recommend a careful viewing of the news any night of the week.

Is this just pessimism? No—it is spiritual realism. We can make progress in politics and education and science and culture, accomplishing wonderful things and improving the lives of many, but we can't shake the effects of sin. We can't solve our problem through an act of the will, for the very compromising and perversion of the will is our problem. It's like someone who is stuck in quicksand: the more you struggle to get out of it, the more you sink into it.

Listen now to the language of the prophet Isaiah, the keynote address for the Advent season: "Behold, you are angry, and we are sinful." St. John Henry Newman said that natural religion wears its dark face outward. The primordial religious experience is this sense of the anger of God. Why? Because we are sinners. So when God comes close, we experience God as angry with us. Now, we should not emotionalize this language, as though God is falling into a snit. The "anger" of God is a way of conceptualizing this experience of alienation from him.

Isaiah continues: "All of us have become like unclean people, / all our good deeds are like polluted rags; / we have all withered like leaves, / and our guilt carries us away like the wind." Notice that Isaiah refers to *good* deeds. He doesn't deny that we can do good things, but he insists that even these are "polluted rags"—which is to say, still tainted by our fundamental dysfunction.

Our language of addiction can help us to understand this truth. When someone finds himself in the grip of an addiction, he is out of control, voiceless. And there is nothing he can do to lift himself out of the problem. This is why, in the twelve-step programs, a person, having hit bottom, must turn his life over to a higher power. He has to surrender to a force beyond his own will, for his own will is the problem. This surrender carries over into his commitment to a group and a sponsor. And this process is usually prompted by some sort of intervention, whereby a group of friends and colleagues breaks through the person's defenses and convinces him that he "needs help."

Furthermore, we know how addictions and other dysfunctions can affect an entire family system. There is a group called Adult Children of Alcoholics, for example, because we realize that people are permanently and deeply affected by the dysfunction of a key family member. A child growing up in a family marked by physical abuse or sexual abuse or substance abuse is permanently marked by the experience. Such a family needs an outside intervention in order to cure it. No one from within the group can solve the problem of the group.

The human race is best characterized as a dysfunctional spiritual family, all of us having been marked from birth by the effects of sin. Sin has found its way into every aspect of human life—personally, societally, and institutionally. We would be hopelessly naïve to think otherwise. And so we need not just a philosopher or social theorist or political activist or military hero; we need a savior, someone who can break into our dysfunction from the outside and heal us.

In light of this discussion, look at the beautiful image with which our Isaiah passage ends: "O Lord, you are our father; / we are the clay and you the potter: / we are all the work of your hands." What we need is the intervention of a loving God who will shape us anew. We can't do it ourselves; we need a savior. When you feel that in your bones, you are ready for Advent.

LOOK TO THE SON OF MAN

Luke 21:25–28, 34–36 (Year C)

Jesus said to his disciples: "There will be signs in the sun, the moon, and the stars, and on earth nations will be in dismay, perplexed by the roaring of the sea and the waves. People will die of fright in anticipation of what is coming upon the world, for the powers of the heavens will be shaken. And then they will see the Son of Man coming in a cloud with power and great glory. But when these signs begin to happen, stand erect and raise your heads because your redemption is at hand.

"Beware that your hearts do not become drowsy from carousing and drunkenness and the anxieties of daily life, and that day catch you by surprise like a trap. For that day will assault everyone who lives on the face of the earth. Be vigilant at all times and pray that you have the strength to escape the tribulations that are imminent and to stand before the Son of Man."

What an extraordinary commencement to the new liturgical year! We are, as it were, slapped in the face with Luke's version of Jesus' apocalyptic speech concerning the end of all things.

"There will be signs in the sun, the moon, and the stars, and on earth nations will be in dismay. . . . People will die of fright in anticipation of what is coming upon the world, for the powers of the heavens will be shaken." This is a kind of unraveling of Genesis. In the beginning, God drew order out of chaos, setting the sun and moon gently in the sky, distinguishing the dry land from the sea, putting our first parents in a peaceful garden.

Jesus predicts the reversal of all of this: the sun and moon will be shaken; the earth will rock and the waves overwhelm the dry land; political order will collapse. But then, in the midst of this chaos, "they will see the Son of Man coming in a cloud with power and great glory." Well, what in the world do we make of this, and why does the Church offer it to us on the first day of the ecclesial new year?

Let's attend first to the imagery of collapse. We hear of cosmic catastrophe—literally a disaster (*dis-astro*, "the falling of the stars"). A sad but undeniable fact of our experience is that nothing lasts. The gorgeous sunset endures for a few minutes, and then it is dark; the sea is placid and calm, but soon it is roiled by great winds; plants grow up, and then they wither and fade; animals in great numbers roam the earth and impress us with their power and beauty, but in a matter of a few years, they fade away. And of course, we, too, come and go. The Psalmist reminds us that our lives are over "like a sigh" (Ps. 90:9).

More to it, we know something about the cosmos as a whole that our ancient brothers and sisters did not—namely, that it, too, is subject to collapse. Aristotle and Plato thought that nature and matter had always existed and would always exist; we know that they came into being at the Big Bang, and scientists argue that it will go out of being at the Big Crunch—or just wear out, growing colder and colder. Everything in the cosmos passes—indeed, even the cosmos itself.

Next, we hear about political chaos: nations will be in tumult. One is tempted to say, "What else is new?" Even the most casual survey of history shows that nations have always been in tumult. Politics has always been a blood sport. Peace is usually just a brief pause between battles, a chance for the two sides to take a breath. Even the Pax Romana of Augustus was bought at a terrible price and lasted only a short time. Much the same can be said of the Pax Americana. Political order comes and goes and is marked at every turn by violence and instability. Wherever human beings are, there will be conflict; this is true at the level of families, corporations, and society.

Some interpret this apocalyptic language as evocative of death, the time when, for all of us, the stars and moon and everything else comes crashing down. We all know in our bones that no matter how much we seek to keep it at bay, death comes to us. For every one of us, at the moment of death, the whole world collapses.

So, do we just fall into depression? No! We realize again the liberating truth that nothing here below lasts; our bodies, politics, nature, the cosmos itself—everything passes. Therefore, don't expect to find your ultimate fulfillment in any of it! Look elsewhere. Look higher.

Now attend to the Gospel once more: "Then they will see the Son of Man coming in a cloud with power and great glory." Jesus is hearkening back to the great prophecy in the seventh chapter of the prophet Daniel. The prophet speaks there of "one like a son of man" who will come on "clouds of heaven" and deliver Israel after a long period of oppression (Dan. 7:13).

This is precisely how the first Christians appreciated Jesus. He was not just one more prophet or teacher. He was the very Incarnation of God's eternal wisdom, God's love, God's way of being. And this meant that he was their link to that eternal power that runs through all things, suffuses all things, transcends all things; that power that endures even when the plants and planets and the cosmos itself fade away; that power that lasts even after our bodies have come and gone.

There is a great tension within Christian thought between the yes and the no. In one sense, there is a great yes to the world, because God made it and made it good. Human beings, political institutions, the world, and the cosmos in its entirety—all of it is good. But here is the no; they are not the ultimate good, precisely because they fade away.

The whole point of this apocalyptic discourse is not to frighten us, but rather to give us hope and to tell us where to look. Don't keep your eyes fixed on the always chaotic and always passing world, on the always unreliable realm of politics, on the fleeting bodily life that we live. Keep your eyes fixed on the Son of Man, who links you to the very power of God.

Watch for him, wait for him, and find your peace in him.

GETTING THE HOUSE IN ORDER

Isaiah 2:1–5 (Year A)

This is what Isaiah, son of Amoz, saw concerning Judah and Jerusalem.

In days to come,
The mountain of the LORD's house
shall be established as the highest mountain
and raised above the hills.
All nations shall stream toward it;
many peoples shall come and say:
"Come, let us climb the LORD's mountain,
to the house of the God of Jacob,
That he may instruct us in his ways,
and we may walk in his paths."
For from Zion shall go forth instruction,
and the word of the LORD from Jerusalem.
He shall judge between the nations,
and impose terms on many peoples.
They shall beat their swords into plowshares
and their spears into pruning hooks;
One nation shall not raise the sword against another,
nor shall they train for war again.
O house of Jacob, come,
let us walk in the light of the LORD!

Christian life has a permanent Advent quality, for we are always expecting the coming of the Lord. There is always a longing, a vigil-keeping that is essential to being a Christian. "Come, Lord Jesus!" (Rev. 22:20).

He came in history, and he will definitively come at the end of time. But he is also coming even now, for the Lord wants to take up residence in us today. Remember how the Lord said to Zacchaeus, "Today I must stay at your house" (Luke 19:5). So Advent is, perhaps most immediately, a preparation for that coming: we are getting ourselves ready to receive the Christ who wants to be born in us.

How do we do this? This passage, taken from the second chapter of the book of the prophet Isaiah, gives us some wonderful instruction. The prophet speaks of the day of fulfillment, the day when the Lord will definitively rule over Israel. Can you see how this is a veiled anticipation of what we will look like when Christ comes to rule over us?

The first thing we hear is this: "In days to come, / the mountain of the LORD's house / shall be established as the highest mountain." This couldn't be simpler—or more challenging. When Christ comes to reign in us, he is the highest value. Period. His house is on the highest mountain. Period. Be honest, something or someone or some value is highest in your life: your career, your wealth, your prestige, your family, your country, your own ego—whatever it might be, everyone has a highest mountain. When Christ comes, he insists on being

Lord of your life, with no competition.

And then Isaiah tells us, "All nations shall stream toward it; / many peoples shall come and say: / 'Come, let us climb the Lord's mountain, / to the house of the God of Jacob.'" Let that beautiful image stay in your mind all throughout the Advent season. The streaming of all the nations of the world toward Jerusalem and the temple is evocative of all the elements of *you* streaming toward Christ: your emotions, your mind, your will, your personal projects and plans, your friendships, your entertainments, your hobbies—everything. It all belongs to him, and he demands to be the Lord of your life. All of us sinners of a religious bent tend to say that Jesus is very important to us; however, if we are honest, he is one interest among many. But Christ is not coming to be one minor interest among others. He will not be sequestered to Sunday alone. He must be the highest value, and everything else in your life must be subordinated to him.

Can I honestly say that every single dimension of my life is under Jesus' lordship? And it doesn't do us one bit of good to play games; we have to be honest with ourselves. If I were to identify a mountain that competes with him, what would it be? A wonderful Advent preparation is just this ordering or reordering of your life. Do what the twelve-step advocates call a searching moral inventory. Go through every aspect of your life that I just mentioned, and ask whether all of them are under Jesus' lordship.

Now, as we continue our reading of Isaiah, here is the good news: "He shall judge between the nations, / and impose terms on many peoples. / They shall beat their swords into plowshares / and their spears into pruning hooks; / one nation shall not raise the sword against another." We are on mysterious ground here, and the prophet is articulating a very important spiritual principle. All of us sinners are at war with ourselves. When Christ is not the center of our lives, we become a jumble of conflicting desires and aspirations. Our public life wants to go this way, but our private life pulls against it. One friendship pulls me here, but another one pushes me there. I have one ideal that brings me this way, but the more realistic side of me goes the other way. My mind seeks this, but my will seeks that. This is the cacophony of the divided self.

But when Christ is the center—when his holy mountain is indisputably the highest—then all of the elements that make us up find harmony, since they are all subordinated to the same end. This friendship will not militate against that one, since both are in service of Christ; my mind will not be at odds with my will, since both are subordinated to the Word; my private life will not conflict with my public life, for both have surrendered their prerogatives to the Lord. The swords will be beaten into plowshares; thus, the weapons of conflict in us now become the means of cultivation. In short, peace will break out in us.

When should all of this happen? *Now!* Listen to Paul as he speaks to the little Christian Church gathered in Rome:

"You know the time; it is the hour now for you to awake from sleep" (Rom. 13:11). In the Bible, sleep is never a good thing; it symbolizes spiritual laziness or inattention. Think, for example, of the disciples sleeping in the Garden of Gethsemane. When should we prepare for the coming of Christ? Now! When should be get our spiritual houses in order? Now! When should we knock down mountains that are higher than the Lord's mountain? Now!

How beautifully the Gospel of Matthew picks up on this motif: "Therefore, stay awake! For you do not know on which day your Lord will come" (Matt. 24:42). Every year, we all dawdle, fall asleep, lapse into spiritual inattention. And every year, when Advent rolls around, the Church shouts at us once more: Wake up! Change! Repent! Prepare the way of the Lord!

INCOMING!

Matthew 24:37–44 (Year A)

Jesus said to his disciples: "As it was in the days of Noah, so it will be at the coming of the Son of Man. In those days before the flood, they were eating and drinking, marrying and giving in marriage, up to the day that Noah entered the ark. They did not know until the flood came and carried them all away. So will it be also at the coming of the Son of Man. Two men will be out in the field; one will be taken, and one will be left. Two women will be grinding at the mill; one will be taken, and one will be left. Therefore, stay awake! For you do not know on which day your Lord will come. Be sure of this: if the master of the house had known the hour of night when the thief was coming, he would have stayed awake and not let his house be broken into. So too, you also must be prepared, for at an hour you do not expect, the Son of Man will come."

Advent (*adventus*) means "coming" or "arrival." Arrivals can be wonderful, joyous, deeply fulfilling—and arrivals can scare the life out of us. Jacques Derrida characterized his famously complex philosophy of deconstructionism as *Viens, oui, oui*, "Come, yes, yes": an openness to the new, the different, the surprising, the incoming. But that last word is telling, isn't it? Soldiers shout "incoming" when missiles and bombs are arriving. Advents can be scary things, for something breaks in to end, upset, or rearrange the current state of affairs.

Listen to the words of the Gospel of Matthew: "Jesus said to his disciples, 'As it was in the days of Noah, so it will be at the coming of the Son of Man.'" These are not very reassuring words. Then he specifies: people were eating and drinking, marrying and being given in marriage, right up to the time of the flood, and then, when it came, with shocking suddenness, they were destroyed.

Our version of Noah's world-destroying flood would be like the crashing of a huge comet into the earth. Scientists tell us that this would destroy civilization and life as we know it. The end of an old world had arrived, but the inhabitants of that world were clueless. A new world was coming, but the prospective citizens of it had no idea how to prepare for it. What if we knew that a comet was coming but did nothing about it? This was the situation of those in Noah's time and, Jesus suggests, those in his own time.

What is so frightening about the coming of the Son of Man? Why isn't it just good news? If he is the life, then life that is opposed to him has to give way; if he is the truth, then false claimants to truth must cede to him; and if he is the way, then the false ways have to be abandoned. And all of this will hurt. If he is the Son of God, then he will break into our sinful world like a cleansing fire, a wild storm, or a violent revolution.

What will this look like? To find out, we turn once more to the prophet Isaiah: "In days to come, / the mountain of the LORD's house / shall be established as the highest mountain / and raised above the hills." The mountain of the Lord's house is Mt. Zion, the place of the temple. In the age of the Messiah, the worship of the living God will be the center and summit of life, the good above any and all goods. From adoration, right order flows. When we worship the true God, we become interiorly and exteriorly ordered. This sounds wonderful, but how will it play in a society in which the vast majority of people have stopped worshiping God—70 percent in the American Catholic Church alone? How will it play out in a world in which sex, pleasure, money, power, and honor are regularly worshiped?

Next we hear that "all nations shall stream toward it; / many peoples shall come and say: / 'Come, let us climb the LORD's mountain / . . . that he may instruct us in his ways.'" In our dysfunction, we like to set up boundaries, divisions, separations. We like to keep our people in and everybody else out. How happy would we be with all nations streaming together to one place? But this is precisely what God wants. More to it, on this mountain, we are all going to take instruction from God. Tell that to the society predicated upon self-assertion and self-esteem, going its own way on its own terms. To say that Jesus is coming is to say that the Lord is coming. How popular will that bit of information be?

"They shall beat their swords into plowshares / and their spears into pruning hooks." This sounds like paradise, but here is a terrible and sobering truth: there would not be so many wars unless—deep down, at some strange, distorted level—we liked them. Think of wars on the grand international level, or think of wars in families and societies. In the distortion caused by sin, we like them. But Jesus tells us to turn the other cheek, resist not evil, bless those who curse you, pray for those who maltreat you.

This is what the coming of Christ the Lord means. It is good news, but in our sin, it's also a time of threat because it means the end of our old world. This is why it involves a complete rethinking and reworking of our lives.

Advent is here; Christ is coming. Are you ready?

THE SECOND WEEK of ADVENT

"Repent, for the kingdom of heaven is at hand!"

—MATTHEW 3:2

REPENT!

Matthew 3:1–12 (Year A)

John the Baptist appeared, preaching in the desert of Judea and saying, "Repent, for the kingdom of heaven is at hand!" It was of him that the prophet Isaiah had spoken when he said:
A voice of one crying out in the desert,
Prepare the way of the Lord,
    make straight his paths.
John wore clothing made of camel's hair and had a leather belt around his waist. His food was locusts and wild honey. At that time Jerusalem, all Judea, and the whole region around the Jordan were going out to him and were being baptized by him in the Jordan River as they acknowledged their sins.

When he saw many of the Pharisees and Sadducees coming to his baptism, he said to them, "You brood of vipers! Who warned you to flee from the coming wrath? Produce good fruit as evidence of your repentance. And do not presume to say to yourselves, 'We have Abraham as our father.' For I tell you, God can raise up children to Abraham from these stones. Even now the ax lies at the root of the trees. Therefore every tree that does not bear good fruit will be cut

> down and thrown into the fire. I am baptizing you with water, for repentance, but the one who is coming after me is mightier than I. I am not worthy to carry his sandals. He will baptize you with the Holy Spirit and fire. His winnowing fan is in his hand. He will clear his threshing floor and gather his wheat into his barn, but the chaff he will burn with unquenchable fire."

During Advent, the Church invites us in a special way to focus on the great figure of John the Baptist. Every detail of John's story is meant to produce an attitude of repentance in us, for it is only through repentance that we are ready to receive the Lord.

Blaise Pascal says that most of our spiritual lives are wasted through *divertissement*—distractions, diversions. We distract ourselves in a thousand ways from the great questions: Who is God? Who am I? What is the purpose of my life? What is the quality of my spiritual life? How is sin affecting me? Where do I stand in relation to eternal life? Instead, we prefer to live in our entertainments and superficialities. Our culture conspires to blind us to these questions and offers us hundreds of excuses to avoid facing them.

Now, we hear that John the Baptist appears in the desert.

What does the desert represent? The desert is the place where our distractions are done away with, where we are stripped down to the basics, where we have to confront the truth about ourselves. That is where the Baptist meets us. And his theme is simple: *metanoiete*. Reform; look; change your mind; change your attitude—all these might be ways of translating that term. The implication is that we are so self-absorbed that we will miss what is most important, what John calls "the kingdom of God." It is most important to note that this kingdom is not a *what* but a *who*. God's way of ordering things has arrived, and we need to wake up, to pay attention. For two thousand years, the Church has echoed John's message, telling the world to pay attention to Jesus, to see what is there to be seen. Jesus is infinitely more than an inspiring teacher or ethical example. Heaven and earth have met; God has come to meet us; God's way and style and substance are now a flesh-and-blood reality.

We hear that "Jerusalem, all Judea, and the whole region around the Jordan were going out to him and were being baptized by him in the Jordan River as they acknowledged their sins." It's a strange paradox, visible up and down the centuries to the present day, that the call to confession is attractive. Deep down, we all know that we are sinners in need of repentance; therefore, the call to confession is not repellent but alluring and compelling. Certainly, in the years that I was coming of age, the language of sin was muted. In the hopes of attracting more people to church, church people stopped talking repentance.

Almost overnight, practice of the sacrament of Confession disappeared. But we know in our bones that confession is good for the soul. In the twelve-step programs, the admission of one's powerlessness is requisite to recovery. Try telling someone going through a twelve-step process that they are just fine the way they are! And so, this Advent, we should hear the message of the Baptist, and like the throngs from Jerusalem and Judea, we should repent and seek forgiveness. This would be a lovely time to go to confession, especially if you have not been for a while. Go to a parish reconciliation service or during confession times, or call your priest and set up a time.

John also presents us with some stark and harsh images. But don't be afraid of them! They are meant to give you life. "Even now the ax lies at the root of the trees. Therefore every tree that does not bear good fruit will be cut down and thrown into the fire." Gardeners knows that plants have to be pruned if they are to thrive. Simply leaving a plant alone will result in its death. Elements that are opposed to its life can develop—not unlike a cancer in the body—and these have to be dealt with promptly and harshly. Part of the process of repentance is the identification of these spiritual anomalies. What needs to be cut down and burned away in you? Hatred, violence, racism, resentments, the inability to forgive, meanness of spirit? All kinds of things grow around the good plant of the spiritual life and threaten to choke God's life in us. Allow God's grace to cut down and burn away all that needs to be destroyed in you.

John continues, "His winnowing fan is in his hand. He will clear his threshing floor." This is an image drawn from the rural life of Jesus' time: the separation of the wheat and the chaff. What is weighty in you and me will remain, while that which is flighty, insubstantial, and trivial will be blown away. Just think of how much chaff there is in us! How much superficiality and stupidity and gassiness, how much fussing around with the ego. Christ wants to blow all of that away.

What is the end result of this going out to the desert, this repentance and confession of sins, this cleansing and purifying? "I am baptizing you with water, for repentance, but the one who is coming after me is mightier than I. . . . He will baptize you with the Holy Spirit and fire." We are meant to be baptized into the divine life. Your life is not about you—thank God! You are meant to be a child of God, a sharer in God's own life. But first, you have to repent.

EDEN, THE HOLY MOUNTAIN, AND THE NEW ADAM

Isaiah 11:1–10 (Year A)

On that day, a shoot shall sprout from the stump of Jesse,
and from his roots a bud shall blossom.
The spirit of the LORD shall rest upon him:
a spirit of wisdom and of understanding,
A spirit of counsel and of strength,
a spirit of knowledge and of fear of the LORD,
and his delight shall be the fear of the LORD.
Not by appearance shall he judge,
nor by hearsay shall he decide,
But he shall judge the poor with justice,
and decide aright for the land's afflicted.
He shall strike the ruthless with the rod of his mouth,
and with the breath of his lips he shall slay the wicked.
Justice shall be the band around his waist,
and faithfulness a belt upon his hips.
Then the wolf shall be a guest of the lamb,
and the leopard shall lie down with the kid;
The calf and the young lion shall browse together,
with a little child to guide them.

The cow and the bear shall be neighbors,
together their young shall rest;
the lion shall eat hay like the ox.
The baby shall play by the cobra's den,
and the child lay his hand on the adder's lair.
There shall be no harm or ruin on all my holy mountain;
for the earth shall be filled with knowledge of the LORD,
as water covers the sea.
On that day, the root of Jesse,
set up as a signal for the nations,
The Gentiles shall seek out,
for his dwelling shall be glorious.

In the second chapter of Isaiah, we hear about God's holy mountain, Mt. Zion: the place of the temple, the place of right worship. Isaiah tells us that peace will break out among us only in the measure that, together, we make the praise of God paramount, with God's mountain raised above all the other mountains and hills. In chapter 11, Isaiah continues the exploration of the Lord's mountain. The mountain that Isaiah describes looks, if you want, both backward and forward: back to Adam and the Garden of Eden and forward to Christ and the heavenly Jerusalem.

God's intention was that we, his human creatures, would live within a watered garden, a place of integration and harmony under the aegis of God's law. Sin is what interrupts this harmony. When Adam and Eve turned from God's ways and arrogated to themselves the prerogative of determining good and evil, they transformed the garden into a desert. God chose a people Israel precisely as a response to this problem. Israel would be a people who would listen to God and worship him and abide by his law. The beauty of their friendship with the Lord would then be a beacon to the rest of the world, bringing everyone to the praise of the true God and restoring the beauty and peace of Eden. This is symbolized in the story of Noah's ark: a floating Eden, if you will, a remnant of God's good order snatched from the sinful world.

The instantiation of Noah's ark in time and space was none other than the temple in Jerusalem, the place of right praise. This is why God's holy mountain is seen as a new Eden. But as every prophet, including Isaiah, tells us, this holy mountain is not altogether holy, and the praise offered in the temple is not altogether righteous. Therefore, Israel began to hope for a priest-king who would definitively preside over the holy mountain and set it utterly right.

Now listen to Isaiah as he prophesies today: "The spirit of the Lord shall rest upon him: / a spirit of wisdom and of understanding, / a spirit of counsel and of strength, / . . . and his delight shall be the fear of the Lord." Isaiah is speaking of the anointed one, the Messiah, who would be a New Adam, a definitive David, a shepherd-king of the holy mountain. Adam took delight in resisting the Lord, but this New Adam will find joy precisely in that surrender. And this will give him wisdom and understanding. In light of his submission to God, he will know what to do and how to live. Further, he will set right what has gone wrong in God's good world, advocating for the poor and smashing the ruthless with the rod of his mouth. "Justice shall be the band around his waist, / and faithfulness a belt upon his hips."

Then watch what happens when this righteous king comes to rule on the holy mountain: "Then the wolf shall be a guest of the lamb, / and the leopard shall lie down with the kid; / the calf and the young lion shall browse together, / with a little child to guide them." Can you see how this is a recapitulation of Eden and of Noah's ark? It is a symbolically charged description of what happens when God is given right praise. When the goods of this world are loved above all, conflict necessarily ensues. But when God is worshiped, then all conflicting parties can find peace. What follows is one of the most beautiful summary statements of the hope of Israel in all of the Bible: "There shall be no harm or ruin on all my holy mountain; / for the earth shall be filled with knowledge of the LORD, / as water covers the sea." This is an image of the Edenizing of the entire world, the whole world having become a temple.

Now flash forward from Isaiah about six hundred years to a very strange figure haunting the Judean desert and eating honey and locusts and wearing camel skin. Isaiah dreamed of the figure who would bring justice to God's holy mountain; John the Baptist sees him around the corner. "Repent, for the kingdom of heaven is at hand!" The kingdom will be concentrated in one great figure. John baptizes with water, but this one will baptize "with the Holy Spirit and fire" (Matt. 3:11); he will dip the world into the power of the divine life. Remember Isaiah's prediction about water covering the sea!

But this process of transformation is not going to be a walk in the park, for the Savior has to set an off-kilter world right. Remember, "He will clear his threshing floor and gather his wheat into his barn, but the chaff he will burn with unquenchable fire" (Matt. 3:12). This is the work of the one who has justice as a belt and righteousness as a band around his hips, the one who will strike the ruthless with the rod of his mouth. This is the Christ, the Anointed, the Son of David, the priest-ruler of the holy mountain, the new and definitive Adam.

GOD HAS REALLY ARRIVED IN HISTORY

Luke 3:1–6 (Year C)

In the fifteenth year of the reign of Tiberius Caesar, when Pontius Pilate was governor of Judea, and Herod was tetrarch of Galilee, and his brother Philip tetrarch of the region of Ituraea and Trachonitis, and Lysanias was tetrarch of Abilene, during the high priesthood of Annas and Caiaphas, the word of God came to John the son of Zechariah in the desert. John went throughout the whole region of the Jordan, proclaiming a baptism of repentance for the forgiveness of sins, as it is written in the book of the words of the prophet Isaiah:

A voice of one crying out in the desert:
"Prepare the way of the Lord,
make straight his paths.
Every valley shall be filled
and every mountain and hill shall be made low.
The winding roads shall be made straight,
and the rough ways made smooth,
and all flesh shall see the salvation of God."

In recent years, a poll revealed that almost half of the people in Great Britain feel that Jesus was not a real historical figure. This is in the land of Edward the Confessor, Thomas More, John Fisher, Edmund Campion, John Henry Newman, and G.K. Chesterton! Needless to say, these figures are rolling their eyes in heaven at this finding.

The historicity of Jesus, the facticity of his life, is of central importance to Christianity. There are many spiritual systems that trade primarily in poetry, myth, and legend, and they use these literary devices to carry their spiritual significance. "Not that there's anything wrong with that!" as Jerry Seinfeld might say. But Christianity is not a mythic system. It is a historical religion that makes very concrete historical claims. Precisely because history is a notoriously inexact science (by definition, its data cannot be reproduced for independent verification), it has scandalized many Christians over the centuries that the faith should rely so heavily upon it. And they have tried, accordingly, to make it into one more mythic expression among many. But the founding texts of our tradition simply do not allow this path of interpretation. The first Christians were intensely interested in the historicity of what they were describing and preaching about.

A particularly good example of this is the Evangelist Luke. Luke was a Greek, most likely a disciple of the Apostle Paul. He writes very polished, elegant Greek—unlike, say, Mark and Matthew—and he explicitly identifies himself as a historian. Look at the prologue to his Gospel: "Since many have undertaken to compile a narrative of the events that have been fulfilled among us, just as those who were eyewitnesses from the beginning and ministers of the word have handed them down to us, I too have decided, after investigating everything accurately anew, to write it down in an orderly sequence for you, . . . so that you may realize the certainty of the teachings you have received" (Luke 1:1–4). This is precisely how an ancient historian would characterize his work. He is not trading in myths and legends—which many authors in the ancient world did, of course. Luke knew this literature, but he emphasizes that he is not writing that sort of book. What he is writing is what people in his time would have recognized as biography.

Now listen to Luke as he commences the great story: "In the fifteenth year of the reign of Tiberius Caesar, when Pontius Pilate was governor of Judea, and Herod was tetrarch of Galilee, and his brother Philip tetrarch of the region of Ituraea and Trachonitis, and Lysanias was tetrarch of Abilene, during the high priesthood of Annas and Caiaphas." Could he get any more exact? Could he be any more completely insistent on situating his story at a particular time and place? Could this be, in a word, any more different from mythic discourse?

All of these figures, by the way, can be independently verified as historical personages. Is Jesus a mythic figure? No! Does it matter for Luke that the things he describes really happened? Yes! Mythic abstractions are fine as far as they go, but they are always susceptible to the charge that they represent wishful thinking, that they are a projection of our own consciousness. Luke is telling us that something *happened*, something so strange and unexpected and rare that it changed everything.

And notice how wonderfully Luke sets us up for the story he will tell. He begins, very much on purpose, the way we would expect an ancient historian to begin: by invoking the high and mighty people. If ordinary folks appeared in history books, they were supporting players or comic relief. This is precisely how, in the next chapter, Luke commences his Christmas story: "When Caesar Augustus was emperor and Quirinius was governor of Syria." But what a surprising move he makes! For the word of God, we are told, does not come to any of these high and mighty players, not even to the high priests in the temple. Rather, it comes to "John the son of Zechariah in the desert." In a word, it comes to the most unlikely person in the most unlikely place. The same will be true, of course, of the Christmas story. The tale is not about Augustus or Quirinius, but about this unknown, poor couple.

Now let us bring this together: history matters so much to Luke because God is intervening to reverse the usual course of history. In many ways, history is a long account of human frailty and folly and wickedness. Empires rise, and empires fall; some good is done, and much evil is done; and round and round it goes. In our myths and stories, we can dream of another world; we can hope against hope that things might be different. But the point of the Gospel is that God has actually intervened in history to turn things around. He has gone around the usual power structures and has made a new world, sending his word first to John, this unlikely prophet in the desert, and then in the flesh in Jesus himself.

Remember that *Adventus* means "coming" or "arrival." The Lord has come; he has really arrived in history. And therefore everything is different.

FINDING THE WAY FROM BABYLON TO JERUSALEM

Isaiah 40:1–5, 9–11 (Year B)

Comfort, give comfort to my people,
    says your God.
Speak tenderly to Jerusalem, and proclaim to her
    that her service is at an end,
    her guilt is expiated;
Indeed, she has received from the hand of the LORD
    double for all her sins.

        A voice cries out:
In the desert prepare the way of the LORD!
    Make straight in the wasteland a highway for
  our God!
Every valley shall be filled in,
    every mountain and hill shall be made low;
The rugged land shall be made a plain,
    the rough country, a broad valley.
Then the glory of the LORD shall be revealed,
    and all people shall see it together;
  for the mouth of the LORD has spoken.

Go up on to a high mountain,
    Zion, herald of glad tidings;
Cry out at the top of your voice,
    Jerusalem, herald of good news!

Fear not to cry out
    and say to the cities of Judah:
    Here is your God!
Here comes with power
    the Lord GOD,
    who rules by his strong arm;
Here is his reward with him,
    his recompense before him.
Like a shepherd he feeds his flock;
    in his arms he gathers the lambs,
Carrying them in his bosom,
    and leading the ewes with care.

Chapters forty through fifty-five of Isaiah—the section that the scholars call "deutero" or "second" Isaiah—were written at the time of the return of the exiles from their captivity in Babylon. For roughly seventy years, the best and brightest of the kingdom of Judah and their descendants had lived far from their sacred homeland in the Babylonian capital.

Imagine what this must have been like, especially for that first generation carried off into captivity. They were forced to live in a land not their own, surrounded by people speaking a strange language and practicing foreign customs. And they were essentially servants, members of an oppressed minority group. No wonder the Psalmist can say, "By the streams of Babylon we sat and wept when we remembered Zion. . . . For there our captors asked of us the lyrics of our songs, and our despoilers urged us to be joyous: 'Sing for us the songs of Zion!' How could we sing a song of the Lord in a foreign land?" (Ps. 137:1–4). Remember a time when you were far from home, when you felt isolated and alone, surrounded by people who were strange to you. Then extrapolate from that, holding in your mind the possibility that you might never escape from that condition.

Now, the point of this prophetic passage from the fortieth chapter of Isaiah is that Israel's exile is coming to an end: "Speak tenderly to Jerusalem, and proclaim to her / that her service is at an end, / her guilt is expiated." God is going to bring his people home. But in order to facilitate this process, some preparation must take place. Between Babylon and Jerusalem stretches a great wilderness, full of hills, valleys, obstacles, rough country. So "a voice cries out: / In the desert prepare the way of the LORD! / Make straight in the wasteland a highway for our God!" Think of rough, mountainous country that stands between you and your destination. How you would long for an eight-lane, beautifully paved highway! And at the end of that highway, upon returning home, they will find the welcoming arms of God: "Here comes with power / the Lord GOD, / who rules by his strong arm. / . . . Like a shepherd he feeds his flock; / in his arms he gathers the lambs, / carrying them in his bosom." What a beautiful image! You are all coming home from exile; a highway will be laid out for you; and God will welcome you, upon your return, with open arms.

Now fast-forward about five hundred years to the alarming figure of John the Baptist, described in the opening lines of the Gospel of Mark: "As it is written in Isaiah the prophet: / *Behold, I am sending my messenger ahead of you; / he will prepare your way. / A voice of one crying out in the desert: / 'Prepare the way of the Lord, / make straight his paths.'*" We find the same language as we found in Isaiah, but this time, the exile in question is not a physical one but a spiritual one. Sin is a wandering away from God, into what St. Augustine called "the region of unlikeness." Sinners, we live in a land far from home, for our home is friendship with God. We are surrounded by people of strange language and customs.

But John cries out in the wilderness that our exile is at an end. He hearkens back to Isaiah's language of the highway that will facilitate the journey from Babylon to Jerusalem. But what exactly is this highway? "One mightier than I is coming after me. I am not worthy to stoop and loosen the thongs of his sandals" (Mark 1:7–8). The highway that fills in the valleys and levels the mountains, the path that facilitates the journey of exiles home to God, is none other than Christ Jesus. How important it is that Jesus refers to himself as the path: "I am the way and the truth and the life" (John 14:6). Thomas Aquinas says that in his divinity, Jesus is the truth and the life, but in his humanity, he is the way.

In Advent, we are meant to move into the psychological and spiritual space of the Babylonian exiles and those spiritual exiles to whom John preached. We are meant to feel what it is like to be far from home, far from where we ought to be. And then we are to rejoice that the path has opened up. We now know how to get from Babylon to Jerusalem, for Christ has laid himself out as a path.

Walk on him, walk in his way, follow after him—and you will find your way home.

THE THIRD WEEK of ADVENT

"The people were filled with expectation."

—LUKE 3:15

“TELL JOHN WHAT YOU SEE AND HEAR”

Matthew 11:2–11 (Year A)

When John the Baptist heard in prison of the works of the Christ, he sent his disciples to Jesus with this question, “Are you the one who is to come, or should we look for another?” Jesus said to them in reply, “Go and tell John what you hear and see: the blind regain their sight, the lame walk, lepers are cleansed, the deaf hear, the dead are raised, and the poor have the good news proclaimed to them. And blessed is the one who takes no offense at me.”

As they were going off, Jesus began to speak to the crowds about John, “What did you go out to the desert to see? A reed swayed by the wind? Then what did you go out to see? Someone dressed in fine clothing? Those who wear fine clothing are in royal palaces. Then why did you go out? To see a prophet? Yes, I tell you, and more than a prophet. This is the one about whom it is written:

Behold, I am sending my messenger ahead of you;
he will prepare your way before you.

Amen, I say to you, among those born of women there has been none greater than John the Baptist; yet the least in the kingdom of heaven is greater than he.”

In the eleventh chapter of Matthew's Gospel, we have moved toward the middle of Jesus' ministry. John the Baptist has been arrested and, having heard about what Jesus is doing, poses a reasonable enough question: "Are you the one who is to come, or should we look for another?" If John asked this question, imagine how many others did as well. When this inquiry is conveyed to Jesus, the Lord does not respond theoretically, but rather by pointing to things that are happening. "Go tell John what you see and hear: the blind regain their sight, the lame walk, lepers are cleansed, the deaf hear, the dead are raised, and the poor have the good news proclaimed to them." Things are happening; things are changing; the desert is blooming.

Was Jesus doing all of this in the literal sense? Yes! That he was a miracle worker and a healer was one of the most fundamental perceptions about Jesus and a prime reason why people were drawn to him. When God came among us in Christ, he effected the work of repairing and restoring his broken, hurting, and dysfunctional creation. He is not simply interested in souls but in bodies as well. And so we hear indeed of the man born blind, of Bartimaeus, of the paralyzed man lowered down through the roof to Jesus, of the woman with the flow of blood, of the man who is deaf and dumb to whom Jesus says "*Ephphatha*!" (Be opened!) (Mark 7:34). We hear of Lazarus and the daughter of Jairus and the son of the widow of Nain.

But the Bible always operates at multiple levels, and all of these physical healings and wonders are meant to be read as evocative of spiritual transformations as well. God cares for bodies, but he also cares for souls! He wants us to have more abundant life at the physical level, but above all, he wants to give us the divine life, the life of grace, a share in the love that God is.

Jesus comes to give sight to blind eyes. How do we read this in a spiritual sense? One of the principal effects of the loss of the divine life is spiritual blindness. Blind people don't know where they're going. They wander more or less aimlessly. The most focused person in the natural order—think of a captain of industry or a leader of business or a military commander—can be utterly lost in the supernatural order. His life can amount more or less to wandering. Grace is a kind of light by which we can see and in which we can walk. Bartimaeus said, "Master, I want to see" (Mark 10:51). And once he regained his sight, he followed Jesus up the road. This is a metaphor for discipleship. All of us sinners are like Bartimaeus: we don't know where we're going; we don't know which road to take. But once we have our sight restored, once the divine light has come into our souls, then we know how to walk in the way of the Lord.

Another principal effect of losing the divine life is spiritual deafness. We can hear every voice but the one voice that matters. We can attend to suggestions from teachers, gurus, pop stars, academics, and newscasters, but we can't attend to the voice of the conscience—what John Henry Newman called the "aboriginal vicar of Christ" in the soul. We can't hear the voice of Christ in the teaching of the Church; we can't hear it in the lives of the saints. But when Jesus gives us the divine life, he restores our hearing. He makes us attentive to the one voice that matters and hence allows us to walk the correct path.

Many people are very, very attentive to lots of different voices in the natural order, responding to all kinds of stimulus and suggestion, but deaf when it comes to the deep things of life. Their life is all about money, or success, or worldly power, or making influential friends. But then they undergo a conversion, and suddenly, through the breakthrough of grace, they hear a different voice, and those concerns just fall away. They become utterly secondary. As Paul says, "I even consider everything as a loss because of the supreme good of knowing Christ Jesus my Lord. For his sake I have accepted the loss of all things and I consider them so much rubbish, that I may gain Christ and be found in him" (Phil. 3:8–9). When the divine life floods into you, your spiritual hearing is restored.

Yet another effect of sin is spiritual lameness or paralysis. I might be the busiest, most active and energetic person in the natural order, but still stuck in place in the supernatural order. I have what the spiritual masters call sloth, or laziness of spirit. But recall that Mary visited Elizabeth "in haste" after the Annunciation. Once we have the divine life in us, we move!

But the principal effect of losing the divine life is spiritual death. This is precisely why the Church speaks of some sins as "mortal"—literally, "deadly" sins. They kill off the love of God in us. They are so repugnant to the manner and purpose of God that they are incompatible with the endurance of the divine life in us. There are lots of walking dead in our culture today; they may be walking around with a clear purpose on the outside, but they are dead on the inside, dead where it matters, dead in relation to God. Grace restores the divine life in us, and this is precisely why the sacraments matter so much. Baptism puts the divine life in us; Reconciliation restores it when it is lost; the Eucharist feeds it; Confirmation strengthens it; Marriage and Holy Orders give it vocational direction; and the Anointing of the Sick prepares it for eternity.

In light of all of this, we can understand a puzzling thing that Jesus says about John the Baptist. He praises him as a prophet, indeed as the greatest of the prophets—and coming from an Israelite, it would be hard to imagine higher praise. John is greater than Isaiah, Jeremiah, Ezekiel, Moses, etc. And yet, "the least in the kingdom of heaven is greater than he." The least in the order of grace is greater than any of the prophets and patriarchs, greater than the greatest of kings, and greater than the greatest of scientists and financiers.

A YEAR OF FAVOR FROM THE LORD

Isaiah 61:1–2a, 10–11 (Year B)

The spirit of the Lord GOD is upon me,
    because the LORD has anointed me;
He has sent me to bring glad tidings to the poor,
    to heal the brokenhearted,
To proclaim liberty to the captives
    and release to the prisoners,
To announce a year of favor from the LORD
    and a day of vindication by our God.

I rejoice heartily in the LORD,
    in my God is the joy of my soul;
For he has clothed me with a robe of salvation
    and wrapped me in a mantle of justice,
Like a bridegroom adorned with a diadem,
    like a bride bedecked with her jewels.
As the earth brings forth its plants,
    and a garden makes its growth spring up,
So will the Lord GOD make justice and praise
    spring up before all the nations.

In Isaiah 61, the prophet declares a year of favor from the Lord. From the time of the Church Fathers, the book of the prophet Isaiah was seen as, *par excellence*, the Old Testament version of the Gospel, for it anticipated so many themes that can be found in the New Testament. One of the most famous is the "suffering servant" motif from chapters fifty to fifty-three, but we also find the motif of the "anointed one." Let's walk through this rich passage, verse by verse.

The text begins, "The Spirit of the Lord GOD is upon me, / because the LORD has anointed me." Now, priests and kings were anointed in the Old Testament, but prophets typically were not. So who is speaking here? I believe the best way to interpret this passage is to see it as an anticipation of the Messiah, the definitively anointed one who will bring salvation. What gives special weight to this interpretation, of course, is that Jesus himself, at the beginning of his public life, chooses precisely this passage in order to present his ministry (see Luke 4:16–21). If we attend to the details of this passage, we can read off very precisely the ministry and meaning of Jesus.

Isaiah continues: "He has sent me to bring glad tidings to the poor." That wonderful phrase "glad tidings" anticipates *euangelion*, the "Gospel." How preoccupied Jesus was with the poor, and how much time he spent with them! Imitating her Lord, the Church has, up and down the centuries, seen service to the poor as one of its central tasks. The corporal works of mercy have a great deal to do with giving concrete aid to the poor. And Jesus also reaches out to those who are spiritually poor, those who are far from God and have lost the sense of meaning and purpose in their lives. He brings to both the economically and existentially poor the good news of God's love. What is this good news? The news of God's journey all the way down into our fallen world. As we read in St. Paul, "You know the gracious act of our Lord Jesus Christ, that for your sake he became poor although he was rich, so that by his poverty you might become rich" (2 Cor. 8:9).

He has been sent, he adds, "to heal the brokenhearted." "Heart," of course, names what is most basic and central to a person, the deepest core of our identity. To be brokenhearted, therefore, is not just to be sad but to be spiritually dysfunctional. We all experience a deep sadness from this compromising of our hearts. In the Beatitudes, Jesus speaks of those who are single-hearted or pure of heart. The brokenhearted might be those whose hearts are compromised. The Messiah has come to heal those broken hearts. He is the *Salvator*, from the Latin *salus*, meaning "health." Jesus has come to heal us at the most fundamental level of our being, to restore us to friendship with God.

He has also come "to proclaim liberty to the captives / and release to the prisoners." One of the greatest metaphors for sin in the Bible is imprisonment. The human soul is meant to fly—out into the world, into the lives of others, and finally into the infinity of God. But egotism and fear lock us into a little soul; Augustine called it *incurvatus in se*, curved into ourselves. Rather than seek relationship with others and friendship with God, I become so preoccupied with my own little concerns that

I lock myself thereby into a prison. Perhaps we could interpret captivity as an indication of addiction—those self-destructive patterns of behavior into which we get caught. The Psalmist cries out, "Lead me forth from prison" (Ps. 142:8). That is exactly what Jesus does through his command to love, even our enemies. How does he do it? By moving right into the place of our imprisonment, to bring the divine mercy and forgiveness and liberation even into those darkest places.

Finally, he has been sent "to announce a year of favor from the LORD." This is a reference to the practice of Jubilee recommended by the book of Leviticus; any first-century Jew would have recognized it. Every fifty years, a great liberation would take place: slaves would be manumitted, and debts would be written off. What beautiful spiritual symbols these are! Slavery and indebtedness are states of being that hang over a person and prevent him from flourishing. Jesus' work would be, primarily, the forgiveness of sins, and sin produces both enslavement and indebtedness. This catches exactly what the first Christians felt like when they were in the presence of Jesus. His cross and Resurrection were a completely unmerited forgiveness of their sins, a relief from their debt, a liberation from their enslavement.

Next, we hear, "I rejoice heartily in the LORD, / in my God is the joy of my soul." I wonder how many of us spontaneously see joy as the whole point of the spiritual life? And how many of us picture Jesus bursting with joy? But he himself said, "I have told you this so that my joy may be in you and your joy may be complete" (John 15:11). God wants us fully alive and sharing in his joy. And how does he make this happen? By clothing the Messiah in "a robe of salvation" and wrapping him in "a mantle of justice." "Salvation" means "healing," and "justice" means "setting things right." In the God-man, sinful humanity is healed of its soul-sickness and put back on line. Think of Jesus wrapping you up in his robe and mantle, conforming you to himself.

Isaiah then gives us the image of "a bridegroom adorned with a diadem." The bridegroom-bride image is a classic one in Scripture and Tradition. Married to Christ, we share in his privileges and prerogatives. We get access to his wealth and his name. The Hebrew behind "adorned with a diadem" clearly indicates that Isaiah is talking about the vesture of a priest, the diadem being his formal turban. Christ is both the Bridegroom and the high priest who has performed a sacrifice on our behalf.

Finally, we hear, "As the earth brings forth its plants, / and a garden makes its growth spring up, / so will the Lord God make justice and praise / spring up before all the nations." The fruit of the Messiah's work is the setting right of the entire world. This is what we are anticipating during the Advent season.

REJOICE ALWAYS!

Philippians 4:4–7 (Year C)

Brothers and sisters: Rejoice in the Lord always. I shall say it again: rejoice! Your kindness should be known to all. The Lord is near. Have no anxiety at all, but in everything, by prayer and petition, with thanksgiving, make your requests known to God. Then the peace of God that surpasses all understanding will guard your hearts and minds in Christ Jesus.

This short passage from Paul's Letter to the Philippians is one of the most significant texts in the entire Bible. It names a truth that is fundamental to the living of the spiritual life.

First, notice how strange it is: "Brothers and sisters: Rejoice in the Lord always. I shall say it again: rejoice!" If someone were to say, "Rejoice when things are going well," or "Rejoice when you're having a good day," or "Rejoice when you landed that job you really wanted," or "Rejoice when you experienced the birth of your first child," we could certainly understand that. But *always*? How could you possibly rejoice when you have had a bitter disappointment, or when you have just gotten terrible news from the doctor, or when you find your fondest dream shattered, or when someone else got that job that you wanted with all your heart, or when you are lying sick in the hospital? And mind you, the grammatical form used by Paul here is the imperative: he is *commanding* us to be joyful. But how can this be? Isn't joy something that comes and goes depending upon circumstances often out of our control? How can you order someone to be happy?

This strangeness signals a pathway to understanding the spiritual truth that Paul is offering. It is indeed the case that the emotional state of contentment—feeling good, being upbeat—cannot be commanded. It is indeed true that these emotions depend largely on factors outside our control, sometimes even on the health of our bodies. It is indeed true that I can feel bitterly disappointed or angry or sad or frustrated in the course of a day. When someone has just received devastatingly bad news, it would be beyond ridiculous for me to say, "Well, be happy!"

So can we leave all of that on one side of the ledger and contrast it with what St. Paul is calling "joy"? Joy has little to do, at the end of the day, with emotions, with having good or bad feelings, with the rush of pain or pleasure that accompanies the changing happenings of the day. Think of those as points on the wheel of fortune. Sometimes you're up, sometimes you're down, and sometimes you're on your way between the two.

But joy is found not on the rim of the wheel, but in the center, where Christ dwells. Joy is not a fleeting emotion, but rather the peace that comes from being grounded in the eternal reality of God. From that place, I can watch the wheel of fortune turn and still be rooted in peace. This is the interior castle of which St. Teresa of Avila speaks, the inner wine cellar that St. John of the Cross describes, the *point vierge* that Thomas Merton evokes. It is the rock referenced in the lyric of an old hymn: "No storm can shake my inmost calm, while to that rock I'm clinging." As the image of a castle suggests, this place is not vulnerable. It is not subject to shifts and changes. The Bible speaks of Jesus as the same yesterday, today, and forever. He is the point of connection to eternity and hence is reliable, firm, absolute. In many ways, the point of the spiritual life is to move from the rim of the wheel to the center—to find this rock, this place of safety, and to live consistently from it.

And this is precisely why Paul could confidently command his readers to rejoice always and in every circumstance. He is not telling them to have positive feelings; he is telling them to reorient their lives to Christ. Notice that he goes on to say, "Have no anxiety at all, but in everything, by prayer and petition, with thanksgiving, make your requests known to God." No anxiety at all? Ever? Didn't Paul himself endure shipwreck, beatings, and imprisonment? Didn't he feel anxious in those moments? Yet the same man who said, "It is no longer I who live but Christ who lives in me" (Gal. 2:20), could indeed say, "I have no anxiety at all." This was not on the level of emotion but on the level of life in Christ.

How do we find this place? How can we respond favorably to the command we have heard on this Gaudete Sunday? This is where prayer comes in. To pray is to raise consistently one's mind and heart to God, to turn intentionally toward God, to clear the space for God to arrive and take root. If I do not pray—and this means the Holy Hour, the Mass, the sacraments, the Rosary, etc.—then almost inevitably my emotions take over and I become prey to all of the changing events of my life.

What enabled Mother Teresa to maintain a spiritual joy in the midst of the worst slum in the world? What enabled Dorothy Day to minister, day in and day out, to beggars and the homeless? What enabled Thomas More to go to his execution joking and laughing? What enabled Walter Ciszek to endure twenty years in the Soviet prison system? Each of these people had found the center. They had responded to the command to rejoice always.

BAPTISM IN THE HOLY SPIRIT

Luke 3:10–18 (Year C)

The crowds asked John the Baptist, "What should we do?" He said to them in reply, "Whoever has two cloaks should share with the person who has none. And whoever has food should do likewise." Even tax collectors came to be baptized and they said to him, "Teacher, what should we do?" He answered them, "Stop collecting more than what is prescribed." Soldiers also asked him, "And what is it that we should do?" He told them, "Do not practice extortion, do not falsely accuse anyone, and be satisfied with your wages."

Now the people were filled with expectation, and all were asking in their hearts whether John might be the Christ. John answered them all, saying, "I am baptizing you with water, but one mightier than I is coming. I am not worthy to loosen the thongs of his sandals. He will baptize you with the Holy Spirit and fire. His winnowing fan is in his hand to clear his threshing floor and to gather the wheat into his barn, but the chaff he will burn with unquenchable fire." Exhorting them in many other ways, he preached good news to the people.

The true transformation of the self—our spiritual elevation into sons and daughters of God—is unique to Christianity. Every decent philosophy, social movement, and religion speaks of moral rectitude, usually under the rubric of justice. All decent people recognize that doing the right thing is essential to human flourishing. Thus, Plato, Aristotle, Cicero, the founding fathers of the United States, Sufi teachers, and Buddhist sages would all speak of moral reform. Indeed, the great prophets of the Old Testament are in that same tradition. Read Hosea, Isaiah, Jeremiah, Amos, Ezekiel—they all call for justice and moral reformation.

John the Baptist is often called the last of the prophets. He is not only last chronologically, but he is also the figure who seems to consistently sum up what is best in the great prophetic tradition. In the beginning of Luke's Gospel, we hear what was probably a typical example of John the Baptist's preaching. Various people come to the Baptist and ask what they must do in order to be more pleasing to God, and he gives them very concrete instruction. To tax collectors, he says, "Stop collecting more than what is prescribed." To soldiers, he says, "Do not practice extortion, do not falsely accuse anyone, and be satisfied with your wages." In other words, he urges the basic works of justice. Like his religious and philosophical colleagues, the Baptist assumes here that this moral reform in the direction of justice can be undertaken through our own efforts. Plato, Aristotle, and Thomas Jefferson would all agree with this—and they would all be right.

But when people suggest that he, the Baptist, might be the Messiah, he quickly and emphatically clarifies the matter. The last and greatest of the prophets says, "One mightier than I is coming. I am not worthy to loosen the thongs of his sandals." Notice something first: we really couldn't imagine, say, Isaiah saying such a thing about Jeremiah, or Amos saying such a thing about Ezekiel. Removing the sandals was something a slave did. While the Old Testament prophets would have respected their successors, it's hard to imagine them saying that they were unworthy to remove their sandals. John is signaling a qualitative difference between himself—and his entire tradition—and this new one who is coming. Something more than a prophet is arriving, and something more than mere moral reform is being predicted.

Notice, too, how the emphasis shifts immediately from things that people can do to things that this new figure will do for them—and to them. "His winnowing fan is in his hand to clear his threshing floor." He himself will do the work of sorting out and cleansing and purifying. Jesus is going to get inside of us and separate the wheat from the chaff, separating what is life-affirming from what is life-denying. And then these decisive words: "He will baptize you with the Holy Spirit and fire." This coming figure will dip people into the fire of God's Holy Spirit—and thereby give them something that they could never otherwise have.

Jesus will not be one more prophet recommending moral reform. He is not against that reform, by any means, but he will effect something more in those he invades, raising them to a level that no philosopher or moral reformer or prophet ever dreamed of. For Jesus is not simply one more prophet, but rather the incarnate Son of God and hence a bearer of the divine life. This life cannot be earned or achieved or merited; it can only be received as a gift. In the classical theology of the Church, this hinges on the distinction between nature and grace. Grace, from the Latin *gratia*, means "gift." Whereas John's commands to his followers speak of taking action, here we move to the passive voice.

Now, what does this invasion of grace, this Baptism with the Holy Spirit, look like? *Baptizein* means to "dip" or "immerse," and the Holy Spirit is the sacred breath breathed back and forth by the Father and the Son; it is the sigh of love eternally exchanged between them, the Love that God is. So to be baptized in the Holy Spirit is to be immersed in the ocean of the divine love. Love is willing the good of the other as other. This is all God can do, since he has no need of anything. God cannot be self-interested. So when we are dipped into this reality, we become capable of something that neither Aristotle nor Plato nor the founding fathers nor the prophets themselves dreamed possible: we can love with the very love of God.

Now look at the saints. To be sure, they are just and prudent and courageous and kind and magnanimous—all of the things that moral philosophers would want them to be. But there is something else in them, something stranger and rarer: they are possessed by a love that they would never, on purely natural grounds, have been capable of. Junípero Serra going to the ends of the world to carry the Gospel; St. Bruno giving himself to utter contemplation of God; Rose Hawthorne taking the dying into her apartment—these things happened because Jesus invaded them and dipped them into the Holy Spirit.

As Christmas Day approaches, welcome this *adventus Christi*.

THE FOURTH WEEK of ADVENT

"Behold, you will conceive in your womb and bear a son."

—LUKE 1:31

BUILDING A HOUSE

2 Samuel 7:1–5, 8b–12, 14a, 16 (Year B)

When King David was settled in his palace, and the Lord had given him rest from his enemies on every side, he said to Nathan the prophet, "Here I am living in a house of cedar, while the ark of God dwells in a tent!" Nathan answered the king, "Go, do whatever you have in mind, for the LORD is with you." But that night the LORD spoke to Nathan and said: "Go, tell my servant David, 'Thus says the LORD: Should you build me a house to dwell in?'

"'It was I who took you from the pasture and from the care of the flock to be commander of my people Israel. I have been with you wherever you went, and I have destroyed all your enemies before you. And I will make you famous like the great ones of the earth. I will fix a place for my people Israel; I will plant them so that they may dwell in their place without further disturbance. Neither shall the wicked continue to afflict them as they did of old, since the time I first appointed judges over my people Israel. I will give you rest from all your enemies. The LORD also reveals to you that he will establish a house for

> you. And when your time comes and you rest with your ancestors, I will raise up your heir after you, sprung from your loins, and I will make his kingdom firm. I will be a father to him, and he shall be a son to me. Your house and your kingdom shall endure forever before me; your throne shall stand firm forever.'"

These words from the second book of Samuel put us in the heart of a deep and abiding mystery of God's providence. Just when we are tempted to say, "Nothing makes sense," the Bible interrupts us to say, "Wait a moment." God works in subtle ways, and often it takes years, even centuries, for his plan to be fully realized. That is why we wait.

In the tenth century BC—a thousand years before Jesus appeared, six hundred years before Plato and Aristotle, and five hundred years before the Buddha—King David is newly established in his palace, his enemies finally subdued on every side, and he turns to thoughts of God's house: "Here I am living in a house of cedar, while the ark of God dwells in a tent!" David wants to construct a great temple for the Lord.

Initially, Nathan, his court prophet, tells him to go ahead, but then Nathan has a dream in which the Lord relates an extraordinary communication. Yes, Yahweh had taken David from the care of his father's flocks to the care of the people Israel, and yes, he had dwelt in a tent from the time of the Exodus, but he does not want David to build him a house. Instead, God turns the tables—in a graceful way: "The LORD also reveals to you that he will establish a house for you." There is a play on words here, for God will not build David a physical house but a dynasty. And then God speaks of this royal house of David, which will last "forever before me; your throne shall stand firm forever." It would be hard to imagine, in the context of the ancient world, a promise more extravagant!

The line of David did indeed last quite a long time, from around the year 1000 BC until the year 587 BC, when the Babylonian conquerors killed the last of David's successors. It had an over-four-hundred-year run, but then it came to a crashing and utterly demoralizing end. To be sure, once the captives returned, they tried to revive the Davidic line, but it didn't work, and other royal lines were established.

Nevertheless—and this is the truly weird thing—ancient Israel remembered the promise that God made to David through the prophet Nathan. 2 Samuel 7 continued to echo in their hearts, even when, to all appearances, it had proved a false promise. Somehow, the hope against hope continued underground, clandestine, hidden away. In fact, the books of Samuel, the scholars speculate, were finally written down in their present form around the year 500 BC—that is to say, after the Davidic line had been broken.

For six hundred years they waited and watched. Then, in

Luke's account of the Annunciation, we hear that the angel Gabriel arrived in a little nothing town called Nazareth in the north of Israel and spoke to a virgin, a very young girl, who was betrothed to a man named Joseph of the house of David. As such, she was considered a member of that house, the house spoken of in the promise made by Nathan. Though the line of kings ended with Zedekiah, the house of David mysteriously endured. Greeting her as "full of grace," the angel announces that she will conceive in her womb and bear a son. "He will be great and will be called Son of the Most High." Then comes the kicker that would have taken the breath away from any first-century Jew listening to the story: "And the Lord God will give him the throne of David his father, and he will rule over the house of Jacob forever, and of his kingdom there will be no end" (Luke 1:32–33).

The seemingly broken promise is not in fact broken. What seemed to have come to an end had in fact just gone underground and was now ready to appear fully in the light. It seemed that the Davidic line had come to an end, that Nathan's prophecy was not true, and that the Lord was not true to his promises. No, says this angel. Now, in the most surprising way, we see the Davidic line continuing through this virgin of Nazareth, betrothed to a man of the house of David, who will give birth to the Son of God, who will have the throne of Jacob and whose reign will last forever. The kingly line of David was in fact unsevered, and now the full meaning of God's promise would be revealed.

God said that he would build a house for David, and David took him to mean his royal line—and this proved to be true as a sort of foreshadowing. But the real house was the body of his Son in which God would be pleased to dwell and into which he would invite the whole world. The house, ultimately, is the Church, which will indeed last forever, because Christ lasts forever and the Church is his Mystical Body. Indeed, the Lord assures us that the "gates of the netherworld shall not prevail against it" (Matt. 16:18).

I fully realize that we are frequently tempted to despair, to say that there is no rhyme or reason to things, that God is not in charge. We are like children who barely sense what their parents are about, who often feel that their parents don't know what they are doing. How can we begin to take in the complexity and mystery of God's design? And so the call is to wait—not hopelessly, but in expectation. The unfolding of his design might not be what we expect or when we expect it, but in an attitude of hopeful anticipation, we wait for its fulfillment. We do not see what God is up to, but we trust.

MARY AS ISRAEL

Luke 1:26–38 (Year B)

The angel Gabriel was sent from God to a town of Galilee called Nazareth, to a virgin betrothed to a man named Joseph, of the house of David, and the virgin's name was Mary. And coming to her, he said, "Hail, full of grace! The Lord is with you." But she was greatly troubled at what was said and pondered what sort of greeting this might be. Then the angel said to her, "Do not be afraid, Mary, for you have found favor with God.

"Behold, you will conceive in your womb and bear a son, and you shall name him Jesus. He will be great and will be called Son of the Most High, and the Lord God will give him the throne of David his father, and he will rule over the house of Jacob forever, and of his kingdom there will be no end." But Mary said to the angel, "How can this be, since I have no relations with a man?" And the angel said to her in reply, "The Holy Spirit will come upon you, and the power of the Most High will overshadow you. Therefore the child to be born will be called holy, the Son of God. And behold, Elizabeth, your relative, has also conceived a son in her old age, and

> this is the sixth month for her who was called barren; for nothing will be impossible for God." Mary said, "Behold, I am the handmaid of the Lord. May it be done to me according to your word." Then the angel departed from her.

As Advent comes to its climax, as the anticipation comes to its fullest expression, the Church invites us to look at Mary. We have seen already two very important Advent figures: Isaiah the prophet and John the Baptist, the last of the prophets. Both are, in significant ways, heralds of the Messiah. But the most important Advent figure is Mary of Nazareth, the Mother of God.

Many years ago, as part of my formation as a seminarian, I was working in a hospital with a group of all non-Catholic students. One day, I brought in my breviary, and one of the Lutheran students picked it up and started paging through it. "You know, you Catholics are really obsessed with Mary," she said, in a kind of playful, provocative way. "I think you put her higher than Christ." I said no, Mary stands to Christ as the moon stands to the sun: she is a reflection of Christ. All of the Marian doctrines and dogmas are Christological in purpose—that is to say, they are meant to draw our attention in some way to Christ. Think of the moon: you can just barely look at the sun for maybe a half second, but you can stare all night at the moon if you want. In a similar way, the intensity of Christ sometimes is overwhelming. But reflected in Mary, we can see, and we can meditate. This is one reason why the Church is continually proposing Mary to us.

What specifically is it about Mary that we are meant to see and be attuned to during Advent? It is this: Mary sums up, in her person, the whole of the people Israel, the nation whose whole purpose was to prepare for the coming of the Lord. In the face of the evil, injustice, stupidity, and sin that were marring his beautiful creation, God resolved to choose a people and to form them according to his heart so that they could be the vehicle of his presence to the world. From this people would come, as a sort of flowering, the Messiah. Thus, Mary recapitulates the story of Israel, the story of redemption. We can, as it were, read the whole Old Testament in her. Let me give but a few examples.

Mary is the New Eve. Eve abandoned paradise when she attempted to cling to godliness, when she arrogated to herself the determination of good and evil, saying, "I am the lord of my own life." On the biblical telling, this was the originating sin, which was then passed on to the whole of the human race, since Eve was the mother of all the living. When we make ourselves the criterion of good and evil, when we make ourselves into God, then we fall apart—and our communities, societies, and ultimately the cosmos itself fall apart too. The great story of Israel is the story of God's steady, relentless, faithful attempt to reverse the momentum of this originating sin by trying to form a people as his friends, as those who would accept his law and his life as gifts and allow themselves to flourish under their influence.

In the great scene of the Annunciation, we see the reversal of this tendency. Hearing the word of the angel, Mary says, "May it be done to me according to your word." Eve, the mother of all sinners, tried to make herself into God. What did Mary do as she reversed the momentum of original sin? Mary acquiesced, surrendered, and agreed to allow God to determine the meaning of her life—and in that moment, she became pregnant with God. Eve's grasping blocked the flow of the divine life; Mary's *fiat*, her acquiescence and acceptance, unleashed it. This is why, as the beautiful medieval commentary has it, the *Ave* (Hail) of the angel is the reversal of *Eva* (Eve).

Mary is also evocative of Moses, and for several reasons. First, she is comparable to the burning bush out of which God's voice addressed Moses. How does God relate to the world? Not invasively, interruptively, or overwhelmingly; rather, the closer God gets, the more we are ourselves. Mary is on fire with the divine presence, with the power of the Word, but she is not consumed by it; she is enlivened by it. "My soul proclaims the greatness of the Lord" (Luke 1:46). Mary, the Church Fathers often said, is like this burning bush because Christ, the divine presence, is alive in her and yet does not overwhelm her, does not suppress her, but rather makes her radiant and luminous.

She is also the new and true Ark of the Covenant. Just as the tablets of the Law were placed within the ark of the covenant as a sign of God's presence to his people, so the Law in person is placed within the Ark of Mary's body. This is why, on the facades of the Gothic churches, Mary and the ark are often pictured together. I used to give tours at Notre Dame Cathedral in Paris, and over the left portal on the facade, there is a depiction of the ark of the covenant and, just above it, a depiction of Mary with the Christ child on her lap. By extension, we could say that Mary is a recapitulation of the temple in Jerusalem. There is a lovely legend that Mary as a young girl was dedicated as a servant in the temple and that she helped to sew the veil of the Holy of Holies. More profoundly, she is, in person, the new Holy of Holies.

More to it, Mary calls to mind that whole series of Israelite women who became mothers against all odds. Think of the unnamed mother of Samson who was infertile; Hannah, the mother of the prophet Samuel, who was childless and prayed that God might give her a son; Sarah, the wife of Abraham, who also was barren and who in her extreme old age gave birth to Isaac; and finally, Elizabeth, her own kinswoman, who was infertile and advanced in years when she became pregnant with John the Baptist. All of these women preach a central biblical truth: new life comes through a stance of radical trust in the Lord, for whom all things are possible. When we are at the end of our strength and at the limit of our hope, God acts. Mary, the

Virgin Mother of God, is the fullest expression of this spiritual archetype.

And in her great Magnificat, Mary is the new Isaiah and the new Jeremiah and the new Ezekiel, for she announces with greatest clarity and joy the coming of the Messiah. What was only vaguely foreseen in those great prophetic figures is now in clear focus:

> "He has shown the strength of his arm,
> and has scattered the proud in their conceit.
> He has cast down the mighty from their thrones
> and has lifted up the lowly.
> He has filled the hungry with good things,
> and the rich he has sent away empty.
> He has come to the help of his servant Israel
> for he has remembered his promise of mercy,
> the promise he made to our fathers,
> to Abraham and his children forever." (Luke 1:51–55)

There is nothing stronger or more beautiful in any of the prophets.

As thc true Israel, Mary knows what to do and does it with enthusiasm. There is no dawdling, backpedaling, straying, or complaining; she simply goes. And she goes upon the heights, which is exactly where God had always summoned Israel, so that it could be a light to the nations.

JOSEPH THE DREAMER

Matthew 1:18–24 (Year A)

This is how the birth of Jesus Christ came about. When his mother Mary was betrothed to Joseph, but before they lived together, she was found with child through the Holy Spirit. Joseph her husband, since he was a righteous man, yet unwilling to expose her to shame, decided to divorce her quietly. Such was his intention when, behold, the angel of the Lord appeared to him in a dream and said, "Joseph, son of David, do not be afraid to take Mary your wife into your home. For it is through the Holy Spirit that this child has been conceived in her. She will bear a son and you are to name him Jesus, because he will save his people from their sins." All this took place to fulfill what the Lord had said through the prophet:

Behold, the virgin shall conceive and bear a son,
and they shall name him Emmanuel,

which means "God is with us." When Joseph awoke, he did as the angel of the Lord had commanded him and took his wife into his home.

The first chapter of the Gospel of Matthew features the intriguing figure of Joseph. Joseph is one of the most beloved of the saints, featured in countless works of art and prominent in the devotional lives of many. One of the greatest devotees of Joseph in recent years was Pope John XXIII. He decreed, during the years of the Second Vatican Council, that Joseph's name be mentioned in the Roman Canon. Yet we know almost nothing about Joseph. There are legends and stories of course, but the scriptural evidence is, to say the least, meager. Yet some very powerful spiritual themes emerge in the accounts of Joseph, all of which focus on the events around the birth of Jesus.

First, we look at the sadness and the quandary of Joseph. He had become betrothed to Mary, and this union had been, according to the religious law of the time, blessed by God. And then he finds that his betrothed is pregnant. There is something terribly universal and contemporary about this scene and about the psychological dynamics involved. An engagement that has to be called off—how embarrassing and difficult that is in itself. What will people say? As a parish priest, I experienced a few instances where couples preparing for marriage called off their engagement. There is something terribly painful about this, no matter what the circumstances are—indeed, even if it was a good decision. Everyone is excited about the wedding, and then suddenly, it has to be called off. The couple has to return their gifts and ask and answer the difficult questions.

But in the case of Joseph, there is more: it has to be called off because of an irregular pregnancy. For someone who is law-abiding and concerned with his status in the community, this would be the profoundest kind of embarrassment. And more to the point, this must have pained him at the deepest emotional level: the feeling of betrayal by one he had loved—a sense of infidelity and unrequited love. What must it have been like to be Joseph in that situation? What must he have felt in his heart? And then push it even further: this was not only a social and psychological trial but a spiritual one as well. Whenever we face a terrible obstacle or tragedy, we wonder, "What is God up to? Why is he allowing this to happen?" All three of these levels of trauma—social, psychological, and spiritual—must have existed for Joseph.

It is a wonderful tribute to the piety and goodness of Joseph that he did not vent his frustration in a way that almost everyone would have understood and countenanced. He swallowed his pain and looked to the feelings of Mary, and, "unwilling to expose her to shame," resolved to divorce her quietly. Then the angel appears to him in a dream and tells him, "Joseph, son of David, do not be afraid to take Mary your wife into your home. For it is through the Holy Spirit that this child has been conceived in her. She will bear a son and you are to name him Jesus, because he will save his people from their sins." Joseph realizes at that moment that these puzzling events are part of a much greater plan of God's. What appears to be a disaster from his perspective is meaningful from God's perspective. "He did as the angel of the Lord had commanded him and took his wife into his home." He was willing to cooperate with the divine plan, though he in no way knew the contours or deepest purpose of it. Like Mary at the Annunciation, he trusted and let himself be led.

When do our lives go off the rails? When we see just as far as our little minds can take us, when we desire just as far as our little wills can carry us, when we live in this little box of what we can see and imagine. The great virtue of St. Joseph was that, at the key moment, he was willing to surrender to a plan and a purpose beyond what he could see or discern. Even though not all of the questions have been resolved, he accepts God's design for his life. Søren Kierkegaard famously wrote, "Faith is a passion for the impossible." Joseph is a great example of this attitude of faith. He plows ahead with this painful and difficult task that God has given him because he knows he is part of a plan that he can't fully understand.

A second aspect of the story is that Joseph listens to God's word in a dream. Dreams play a very interesting role in the Bible. Jacob has a dream while sleeping on the stone and sees the angels ascending and descending; the Old Testament Joseph is an interpreter of dreams and successfully reads the dream of Pharaoh; the wise men in the New Testament are redirected to their homeland because an angel appears to them in a dream. In one of the Psalms, we find this line: "Even in the night my heart exhorts me" (Ps. 16:7). In the stories of the saints, there are numerous references to God speaking through dreams. Many artists and scientists have told us that their inspiration has come from dreams. When Freud and Jung in the twentieth century speculated that dreams are the bearers of deep meanings, they were speaking out of a very old tradition.

What does it mean that Joseph is willing to listen to the wisdom of a dream? It means that he is willing to go beyond the strictures of the rational mind—not repudiating them, but going beyond them, thinking in new ways, entertaining unexpected possibilities, plumbing deeper and richer dimensions of his soul. It is an openness to a way of knowing, a way of seeing, which is beyond the ordinary. A lot of spiritual masters say that one of our basic problems is that we get stymied by rationalism. The Bible and the Church never recommend that we repudiate reason; the problem comes when we say that the only thing that is real is what we can know by reason. Then we live in a very tight and controlled and narrow space, and we are unable to hear the word of God when it comes. We can't see the patterns of God when they emerge. Faith is a willingness to dream in that sense. It is a willingness to be challenged out of our ordinary way of seeing and relating.

Think of the Christmas story: God becomes one of us. In order to save us from our sins, he becomes a little baby. Common sense? Hardly. Corresponding to what we normally see and think about? No. Only dreamers believe it—and I don't mean that in the pejorative sense. I mean those who have a mind and heart expansive enough to take in God's ways, God's mind, God's way of seeing. As we approach the Nativity of the Lord, we are encouraged to dream, like St. Joseph, according to the rhythms and the patterns of God's own mind. In that way, we are more ready for Christ's coming.

SON OF DAVID, SON OF GOD

Luke 1:39–45 (Year C)

Mary set out and traveled to the hill country in haste to a town of Judah, where she entered the house of Zechariah and greeted Elizabeth. When Elizabeth heard Mary's greeting, the infant leaped in her womb, and Elizabeth, filled with the Holy Spirit, cried out in a loud voice and said, "Blessed are you among women, and blessed is the fruit of your womb. And how does this happen to me, that the mother of my Lord should come to me? For at the moment the sound of your greeting reached my ears, the infant in my womb leaped for joy. Blessed are you who believed that what was spoken to you by the Lord would be fulfilled."

I have always been fascinated by Mary's "haste" in the story of the Visitation. Upon hearing the message of Gabriel concerning her own pregnancy and that of her cousin, Mary "traveled to the hill country in haste to a town of Judah" to see Elizabeth.

Why did she go with such speed and purpose? Because she had found her mission, her role in the theo-drama. We are dominated today by the ego-drama in all of its ramifications and implications. The ego-drama is the play that I'm writing, producing, directing, and starring in. We see this absolutely everywhere in our culture. The watchword today is tolerance, which translates as "You let me do what I want to do, and I will let you do what you want to do—as long as we don't hurt each other." Freedom of choice reigns supreme: I become the person that I choose to be. Any claim to objective truth or goodness is written off as a power move, the imposition of an alien will. Look, for example, at the work of Friedrich Nietzsche, who is the most influential philosopher of the nineteenth century, primarily because of his philosophy of "the will to power." Everything is reduced to power and the play of power.

What the ego-drama produces is the "meh culture." "Meh"—who cares? No one has a purpose beyond the one that he or she makes up. Now, there is something deeply alluring about awakening to a sense of freedom, and young people feel it especially as they are coming of age. But you really begin to live when something grabs your will from the outside and gives it direction, when something so compels you and fascinates you that you want to give your whole life to it. Then you are no longer just making it up on your own; rather, you have been chosen. That is why the Lord says, "It was not you who chose me, but I who chose you" (John 15:16). It is like John Henry Newman's distinction between the river with firm banks and the lazy lake. A river with firm banks has energy and verve and direction. If, Newman says, we knock down the banks in the name of "freedom," that purposeful and energetic river opens up into a big lazy lake. But then it is as if we are all floating around on our own individual tubes. We have no verve, no zest, no spiritual purpose. The classical spiritual masters referred to this condition as the deadly sin of sloth.

Contrast this to the theo-drama. The theo-drama is the great story being told by God, the great play being directed by God in which he wants to involve you. What makes life thrilling is to discover your role in it. This is precisely what has happened to Mary. She has found her role—indeed a climactic role—in the theo-drama, and she wants to conspire with Elizabeth, who has also discovered her role in the same drama. Mary does not get it entirely, does not see every aspect of it, and is not in control of it. But she surrenders to it and accepts it; this is what gives her verve and energy and purpose, and it is why she goes in haste into the hill country. She is not just floating on the lazy lake of the ego-drama; she has been gripped by the theo-drama.

Notice, with the lazy lake image in mind, how the ego-drama drives us apart—and you can see it everywhere today in our hyper-litigious and rights-oriented culture. How often we fall into an "us against them" stance. But the theo-drama draws us together, for it shows how we are all part of something greater than any one of us. Real friendships, Aristotle tells us, commence when the two friends together fall in love with a "transcendent third," some great good that goes beyond both of them. The ego-drama is not enough to sustain real, strong relationships;

what is needed is a common surrender to the demands and excitement of the theo-drama. We are drawn together more closely when we rise above our egotism and together fall in love with some value beyond ourselves. It is precisely in this spirit that Mary and Elizabeth come together with such joy and with such a sense of spiritual purpose. Together, they have fallen in love with God's story.

Now, what precisely is the story of which they are a part? We have to go back to the Old Testament to see the full sweep of it. King David had gathered the tribes of Israel, united the nation, and then established a capital not far from his birthplace, a city called Jerusalem. And into that city he brought the central symbol of Israelite religion, the ark of the covenant, dancing with abandon before it. Later, the prophet Micah prophecies of a son of David who would come from David's city of Bethlehem and reign as the Messiah: "He shall stand firm and shepherd his flock / by the strength of the LORD, / in the majestic name of the LORD, his God; / and they shall remain, for now his greatness / shall reach to the ends of the earth; / he shall be peace" (Mic. 5:3–4). Micah is clearly talking about a human figure, but he is also insinuating that this king would not be an ordinary king, just one more in a long line of the descendants of David. This son of David also, strangely, is the bearer of God's power and authority. We can see this motif all over the Old Testament. On the one hand, a son of David will be the Messiah, but on the other hand, God himself will come and shepherd his people.

David's bringing of the ark into the city of Jerusalem has a parallel with the Visitation. Mary comes into the hill country of Judah—and that is exactly where David found the ark of the covenant: in "the house of Abinadab on the hill" (2 Sam. 6:3). Mary is the new Ark of the Covenant. The original ark contained the Ten Commandments, the Word of God; in her own womb, Mary carries the Word of God made flesh. How wonderful, too, that David dances before the ark; likewise, the infant John the Baptist, leaping in his mother's womb, does his own sort of Davidic dance before the true Ark of the Covenant. And finally, attend to what Elizabeth says to Mary when the maid of Nazareth pays her a visit: "And how does this happen to me, that the mother of my Lord should come to me?" This again echoes the words of David: "How can the ark of the LORD come to me?" (2 Sam. 6:9). Elizabeth recognizes the deep truth before her: the baby gestating in Mary's womb is not just a human king-to-be, but is, somehow, Adonai, the Lord, the God of Israel.

CHRISTMAS DAY

"And the Word became flesh and
made his dwelling among us."

—JOHN 1:14

THE WORD BECAME FLESH

Matthew 1:1–25 (Vigil Mass)

The book of the genealogy of Jesus Christ, the son of David, the son of Abraham.

Abraham became the father of Isaac, Isaac the father of Jacob, Jacob the father of Judah and his brothers. Judah became the father of Perez and Zerah, whose mother was Tamar. Perez became the father of Hezron, Hezron the father of Ram, Ram the father of Amminadab. Amminadab became the father of Nahshon, Nahshon the father of Salmon, Salmon the father of Boaz, whose mother was Rahab. Boaz became the father of Obed, whose mother was Ruth. Obed became the father of Jesse, Jesse the father of David the king.

David became the father of Solomon, whose mother had been the wife of Uriah. Solomon became the father of Rehoboam, Rehoboam the father of Abijah, Abijah the father of Asaph. Asaph became the father of Jehoshaphat, Jehoshaphat the father of Joram, Joram the father of Uzziah. Uzziah became the father of Jotham, Jotham the father of Ahaz, Ahaz the father of Hezekiah. Hezekiah became the father of Manasseh, Manasseh the father of Amos,

Amos the father of Josiah. Josiah became the father of Jechoniah and his brothers at the time of the Babylonian exile.

After the Babylonian exile, Jechoniah became the father of Shealtiel, Shealtiel the father of Zerubbabel, Zerubbabel the father of Abiud. Abiud became the father of Eliakim, Eliakim the father of Azor, Azor the father of Zadok. Zadok became the father of Achim, Achim the father of Eliud, Eliud the father of Eleazar. Eleazar became the father of Matthan, Matthan the father of Jacob, Jacob the father of Joseph, the husband of Mary. Of her was born Jesus who is called the Christ.

Thus the total number of generations from Abraham to David is fourteen generations; from David to the Babylonian exile, fourteen generations; from the Babylonian exile to the Christ, fourteen generations.

Now this is how the birth of Jesus Christ came about. When his mother Mary was betrothed to Joseph, but before they lived together, she was found with child through the Holy Spirit. Joseph her husband, since he was a righteous man, yet unwilling to expose her to shame, decided to divorce her quietly. Such was his intention when, behold, the angel of the Lord appeared to him in a dream and said, "Joseph, son of David, do not be afraid to take

> Mary your wife into your home. For it is through the Holy Spirit that this child has been conceived in her. She will bear a son and you are to name him Jesus, because he will save his people from their sins." All this took place to fulfill what the Lord had said through the prophet:
> *Behold, the virgin shall conceive and bear a son,*
> *and they shall name him Emmanuel,*
> which means "God is with us." When Joseph awoke, he did as the angel of the Lord had commanded him and took his wife into his home. He had no relations with her until she bore a son, and he named him Jesus.

"The Word became flesh / and made his dwelling among us." But in order fully to appreciate the implications of that somewhat abstract statement from St. John's prologue, it is useful to reflect on St. Matthew's account of the genealogy of Jesus, which begins with these words: "The book of the genealogy of Jesus Christ, the son of David, the son of Abraham." Matthew will show precisely what it means for the Word of God truly to become flesh, to enter into a human family, with all of its ambiguities and foibles. Because of the Incarnation, it is accurate to say that God had a grandmother, cousins, weird uncles, and eccentric aunts. In fact, in the long list of Jesus' ancestors provided by

Matthew, we can see saints, sinners, cheats, murderers, poets, kings, insiders, and outsiders—all leading to the Christ. The good news is that, as Christ came forth precisely from this dysfunctional family, so Christ can be born in us, in the midst of our ambiguous, dysfunctional families.

Matthew originally wrote for a Jewish audience, and they would have been very familiar with these names and known their stories. It would be a bit like speaking to an American audience of Washington, Adams, Jefferson, Franklin, Hamilton, and Lincoln. So let's consider just a few of these ancestors.

We know Jacob, the grandson of Abraham, who became the father of twelve sons, the patriarchs of the twelve tribes of Israel. But he was also the one who tricked his brother Esau out of his birthright. He had the marvelous dream of a ladder connecting heaven and earth, with angels of God ascending and descending upon it. After wrestling with God in that marvelous story, Jacob was wounded, affected physically for the rest of his life. Maybe all your life you have been wrestling with God—doubting, questioning, wondering what he is about. Believing in God, yes, but still struggling to understand, struggling to accept. Maybe you have been wounded by this struggle. Well, Christ came forth from this ancient wrestler with God; he was pleased that he was one of his ancestors. Maybe Christ can be born in the Jacobs of today.

Someone else who we rarely attend to is Ruth, a Moabite woman who married into the family of an Israelite and remained loyal to it even after her husband died. You can read her story in the book of Ruth, which is maybe only five pages and appears between the book of Judges and 1 Samuel. Naomi and her two sons wandered from Israel into the land of the Moabites, and one of her sons married Ruth. They all lived together for a number of years, until finally the son died. Naomi decided to return to Israel but told Ruth to stay with her own people. Ruth, however, said no: "Wherever you go I will go, / wherever you lodge I will lodge. / Your people shall be my people / and your God, my God. / Where you die I will die, / and there be buried" (Ruth 1:16–17). So she returned with Naomi. Where did they come back to? To a little town called Bethlehem. She then married a man named Boaz, mentioned in the genealogy, and became the mother of Obed, who became the father of Jesse, who sired a boy named David. The key point is that Ruth was an outsider, but Christ was pleased to have her as his ancestor. It was a foreigner who became the great-grandmother of Israel's greatest king. I bet there are many reading this right now who maybe have felt like Ruth: something of an outsider, something of a foreigner, not quite fitting in. Well, from you, Christ can come. Perhaps from your very exclusion God is working out his will.

Rahab, too, is mentioned as an ancestor of Christ. If St. Matthew was interested in preserving the respectability of Jesus' family line, he would have found a way to eliminate her from the genealogy. Who was Rahab? You can read her story in the book of Joshua. She was a prostitute in the town of Jericho during the time of the Israelite invasion of the Promised Land. She sheltered two Israelite spies and hence was spared when the Israelites destroyed Jericho. Maybe there are people reading this right now who feel something like Rahab. You may feel unworthy—that certain things you have done are so bad that God could never forgive you. But Christ was pleased to have Rahab as one of his ancestors. Even from this compromised sinful figure, salvation can come forth.

Of course, King David is mentioned. He was, without doubt, a magnificent figure: the king who united the nation, defeated its enemies, and established the first Israelite empire. But he was also, we know, an adulterer and a murderer, the one who abused his power in order to eliminate Uriah the Hittite. Lest we forget this, Bathsheba, the woman with whom David had his adulterous affair, the woman who betrayed her husband Uriah, is indirectly mentioned in the genealogy as the mother of Solomon. And speaking of Solomon: he was, like his father, a great king, the wisest man in history, and the builder of the temple in Jerusalem. But he was also an adulterer and an idolater whose sins led to the breakup of the Israelite nation. I bet there are some people reading this who feel like David or Solomon: big dealers, important players, kings of family or industry or work, those who stride confidently onto the stage—but also those who harbor private sins, who sometimes abuse their power and position and authority, who are secretly afraid. From you and in you, Christ can be born.

We hear of Jechoniah, who was king at the time of the Babylonian captivity. He was an evil man and was placed under a curse by Jeremiah. He and his family were carried off into exile by the Babylonians in absolute humiliation. I bet there are some people reading this who feel like Jechoniah: a failure, the inheritor of a great tradition and a great name whose whole world fell apart. From you and in you, Christ can be born.

We hear of Abiud, Eliakim, Azor, and Zadok. Who were they? We know almost nothing about them. Even the great specialists in the Bible have no idea who these figures are. They were more or less hidden characters, lost in the mists of history. I would be willing to bet that there are some people reading this who feel like Abiud, Eliakim, Azor, and Zadok: unsung, unaccomplished, unknown, unappreciated. Well, the Messiah was pleased that these forgotten figures were among his ancestors. And yes, even from the very simplicity of those of us who feel unsung and unappreciated, Christ can be born.

From this long line of great and not-so-great, prominent and obscure, saints and sinners, kings and paupers came "Jesus who is called the Christ." God became one of us, in all of our grace and embarrassment, in all of our beauty and ordinariness. God had a series of human ancestors, and, like most families, they were kind of a mixed bag. What good news this is for us, and what great comfort we can take from it! It means that God can bring Christ to birth even in such as ourselves.

Trust not in your own powers and status and worldly attainments. Trust in the grace that writes straight with our crooked lines. Trust in that power that presides over the mess and muck of the human condition—and brings Christ to birth.

CHRIST-MASS

John 1:1–18 (Mass during the Day)

In the beginning was the Word,
  and the Word was with God,
  and the Word was God.
 He was in the beginning with God.
 All things came to be through him,
  and without him nothing came to be.
 What came to be through him was life,
  and this life was the light of the human race;
 the light shines in the darkness,
  and the darkness has not overcome it.

A man named John was sent from God. He came for testimony, to testify to the light, so that all might believe through him. He was not the light, but came to testify to the light. The true light, which enlightens everyone, was coming into the world.

 He was in the world,
  and the world came to be through him,
  but the world did not know him.
 He came to what was his own,
  but his own people did not accept him.

But to those who did accept him he gave power to become children of God, to those who believe in his name, who were born not by natural generation nor by human choice nor by a man's decision but of God.

And the Word became flesh
and made his dwelling among us,
and we saw his glory,
the glory as of the Father's only Son,
full of grace and truth.

John testified to him and cried out, saying, "This was he of whom I said, 'The one who is coming after me ranks ahead of me because he existed before me.'" From his fullness we have all received, grace in place of grace, because while the law was given through Moses, grace and truth came through Jesus Christ. No one has ever seen God. The only Son, God, who is at the Father's side, has revealed him.

Our Gospel for Christmas Day is, of course, one of the most famous texts in the entire Bible: the prologue to the Gospel of John. In many ways, it is the entire Gospel, indeed the entire Bible, in miniature. So it rewards a careful reading.

"In the beginning was the Word, / and the Word was with God, / and the Word was God." St. John is purposely drawing our attention back to the very first word of the entire Bible:

bereshith, "in the beginning." Jesus is going to be the culmination of the great story of creation—a new creation, a renewal and a starting afresh. God is always about the business of doing something new!

And in the beginning was "the Word"—*davar* in Hebrew, *logos* in Greek. The Old Testament insists on the presence of the Word from the beginning when it says that God speaks the world into existence: "Let there be light," and there was light; "Let the dry land appear," and so it did; etc. The universe is not just absurdly there; since God speaks the world into existence, it is filled with intelligibility, order, harmony, and purpose. "All things came to be through him, / and without him nothing came to be." All the sciences depend on this assumption that the universe is marked by intelligibility. Order and harmony are placed in things by God, and human beings are given the task of recognizing this intelligibility in both the intellectual and the moral order: "This life was the light of the human race." At our best, we are like priests and prophets, honoring God and naming the truth that he has placed in things. Eden was meant to be a sort of temple, a place of right relationship between human beings and God.

So what is sin on the biblical reading? What went wrong? One way to express it is as a refusal to acknowledge this Word, a refusal to live in line with the intellectual and moral intelligibility available in God's universe. Put this in terms of the biblical image of Genesis 3: it is to grasp at the tree of the knowledge of good and evil. It is to arrogate to oneself the prerogative of creating light. Do you think this is all abstract? Think again. Sin remains fundamentally the same across the ages. Today, claiming for ourselves the prerogative of God takes the form of self-invention: I decide the meaning of my life, of my body, of the world itself.

To address this difficulty, God formed a people after his own heart, a people who would be prophetic and priestly, who would know how to speak the truth about him and would know how to order their lives according to right praise. This is why he established a priesthood, a liturgy, and a temple. The great temple in Jerusalem, constructed by King Solomon, was meant to be a little Eden, a place where God is rightly praised, a microcosm of the world filled, as it should be, with the glory of God. Since it was the descendent of the great tent or tabernacle that the Israelites built in the desert when they were sojourning from Egypt, the temple is sometimes called the tabernacle.

With all of this in mind, let us turn to verse 14, the central passage of John's prologue: "And the Word became flesh / and made his dwelling among us." The word used in Greek here for "dwelt" is *eskenosen*, which means literally "pitched his tent among us." Don't read that in a folksy way; it is meant to call to mind the tabernacle of the temple. The Word becoming flesh is God coming to dwell definitively in his world, undoing the effects of sin and turning it into what it was always meant to be. Notice, too, what we see in the wake of this tabernacling: "And we saw his glory, / the glory as of the Father's only Son, / full of grace and truth." The Greek word *doxa* used here is a rendering of the Hebrew *shekinah*, which means "light" or "glory" or "weight." This was the word used to describe the presence of the Lord dwelling in the tabernacle and in the temple. The place of right praise becomes like the burning bush: a radiant vehicle of the divine presence. So John is telling us that Jesus is the new Eden, the new Temple, the restored creation, the realization of God's intention for the world. And our purpose is not simply to gaze on this fact with wonder, but rather to enter into its power: "From his fullness we have all received, grace in place of grace."

Here is a point that, at least in my lifetime, has rarely been reflected upon: this feast is called "Christmas" because it signals Christ's Mass. Where precisely is the new Temple, the new Eden, the restored creation, on display? The Mass, which is, *par excellence*, the place of right praise. Where do we receive the divine life, grace upon grace? At the Mass. Where is the power of the Incarnation most vividly visible? At the Mass. Where do we encounter the tabernacling of God in the midst of his people? At the Mass.

What, therefore, is the very best way to celebrate the Incarnation? Go to Mass!

A BABY IN STRAW POVERTY

Isaiah 9:1–6 (Mass during the Night)

The people who walked in darkness
have seen a great light;
Upon those who dwelt in the land of gloom
a light has shone.
You have brought them abundant joy
and great rejoicing,
As they rejoice before you as at the harvest,
as people make merry when dividing spoils.
For the yoke that burdened them,
the pole on their shoulder,
And the rod of their taskmaster
you have smashed, as on the day of Midian.
For every boot that tramped in battle,
every cloak rolled in blood,
will be burned as fuel for flames.
For a child is born to us, a son is given us;
upon his shoulder dominion rests.
They name him Wonder-Counselor, God-Hero,
Father-Forever, Prince of Peace.
His dominion is vast
and forever peaceful,
From David's throne, and over his kingdom,

which he confirms and sustains
By judgment and justice,
both now and forever.
The zeal of the LORD of hosts will do this!

I once read an interview in *Rolling Stone* magazine with Bono, the lead singer of the group U2 and a celebrated philanthropist. In the course of this wide-ranging interview, Bono was asked about his faith. After clarifying that the Bible is the book that "sustains" him, he said this about his faith in God: "I believe there's a force of love and logic in the world, a force of love and logic behind the universe. And I believe in the poetic genius of a creator who would choose to express such unfathomable power as a child born in 'straw poverty.'" The power that creates the cosmos, the order that stands behind all things, is best expressed as humble, compassionate love. That is the revolution at the heart of our faith; that is the Christmas message.

Peace—*shalom*—was the abiding dream of Israel. In that word are summed up a number of ideas: justice, right order, fellowship, peace. Yet from the very beginning, there was murder: Cain put his own brother to death and then became the founder of cities—meaning that behind our human conception of order, there is violence, domination, manipulation, control. What follows is the chaos that led to the flood; the bickering of the Tower of Babel; the feud between Abraham and Lot; the rivalry of Jacob and Esau; the hatred of Joseph in his brothers; the enslavement of Israel by the Egyptians; the endless wars of conquest with the Philistines, the Canaanites, and the Jebusites; the conquest of Israel by Assyria, Babylon, Greece, and Rome; the revolt of the Maccabees. The ancient Israelites were a people well acquainted with war; the Bible is a book of battles. But through it all, how they longed for *shalom*!

Throughout the telling of this story, there are wonderful dreamers who begin to dream of a different way, a different order, a different kingdom. Isaiah the prophet sums up these two sides of the Israelite experience. "The people who walked in darkness / . . . upon those who dwelt in the land of gloom / . . . the yoke that burdened them, / the pole on their shoulder, / and the rod of the taskmaster." There is summed up the warfare, the oppression, the violence that so sadly characterize Israel and the world. But in the midst of this, they maintained a hope that, one day, God would gather the tribes of Israel into a peaceful nation, a priestly people, and that through this holy nation he would in turn gather all of the tribes of the world into a family marked by love and justice.

In Isaiah we hear a peculiar expression of that hope, in the measure that it focuses on a child: "For a child is born to us, a son is given us; / upon his shoulder dominion rests." Through him the tribes of Israel would be gathered. And then his names: "Wonder-Counselor, God-Hero, / Father-Forever, Prince of Peace." Every other prince the world has ever known has been a prince of war, maintaining his authority through violence. But Isaiah dreams of this child king whose "dominion is vast and forever peaceful, / from David's throne, and over his kingdom." This child is the one through whom Israel would become a great and peaceful nation and, by extension, through whom the whole world would be gathered.

It is against this rich and loamy background that we must read the familiar Christmas account in Luke's Gospel. It begins by invoking the most powerful king in the world, the commander of the greatest army the world had ever known, the one who imposed an order on the empire through the threat of violence: Caesar Augustus. Augustus had come to power in that confusing time after the assassination of Julius Caesar and a terrible civil war. Was he a "prince of peace"? Hardly. He was a typical worldly ruler: canny, pragmatic, ruthless. Because of his decree—a census that would make his world easier to control—people from all over his empire were forced to move. Accordingly, Mary and Joseph made their way from Nazareth to Bethlehem, from one nothing town to another. If you had mentioned either town to Caesar Augustus, he would have given you a blank stare.

There a child is born. There is no room at the inn, so he is laid in a manger, wrapped in swaddling clothes, warmed by the breath of the animals. The love and the logic that created the universe is revealed not in the power games and power struggles that characterize almost the whole of human history, but in the straw poverty of this baby, too weak to hold up his own head. In this child, the truth becomes clear: God's power, the order that makes the whole universe, is self-emptying love—vulnerable, compassionate love. The fallen world is governed by Caesar and his minions—people who are powerful, well-fed, living in palaces, and imposing their will on their enemies. But the one whom the shepherds found looks nothing like that. He is lying in a manger, the place where animals eat, situated in a miserable barn or cave; he can't impose his will on anyone, for he is utterly helpless. But that is what the Savior, the Lord, looks like, for he is the one who overturns the powers of this world.

Isaiah, it turns out, was right: the *shalom* that Israel longed for throughout its whole history appeared as a little child, the Prince of Peace. It is a poetic reversal effected by that logic that stands behind all of creation, which turns all of our human expectations upside down. Do you want to unleash the power of heaven? Do you want God's order, God's kingdom, to be made present on earth as in heaven? Then don't follow Caesar; follow this baby King.

THE MESSAGE OF THE ANGELS

Luke 2:1–14 (Mass during the Night)

In those days a decree went out from Caesar Augustus that the whole world should be enrolled. This was the first enrollment, when Quirinius was governor of Syria. So all went to be enrolled, each to his own town. And Joseph too went up from Galilee from the town of Nazareth to Judea, to the city of David that is called Bethlehem, because he was of the house and family of David, to be enrolled with Mary, his betrothed, who was with child. While they were there, the time came for her to have her child, and she gave birth to her firstborn son. She wrapped him in swaddling clothes and laid him in a manger, because there was no room for them in the inn.

Now there were shepherds in that region living in the fields and keeping the night watch over their flock. The angel of the Lord appeared to them and the glory of the Lord shone around them, and they were struck with great fear. The angel said to them, "Do not be afraid; for behold, I proclaim to you good news of great joy that will be for all the people. For

> today in the city of David a savior has been born for you who is Christ and Lord. And this will be a sign for you: you will find an infant wrapped in swaddling clothes and lying in a manger." And suddenly there was a multitude of the heavenly host with the angel, praising God and saying:
>
> "Glory to God in the highest
> and on earth peace to those on whom his favor rests."

For most people, the presence of angels in the Christmas story is just a charming decoration to the main narrative and not essential to it. I suppose this prejudice is born of thousands of saccharine depictions of angels on Christmas cards. But the angels are actually at the heart of the matter, and the word used to describe these heavenly beings gives away the game: *angeloi*, which simply means "messengers." The angels of Christmas are messengers carrying a word from a higher world to this world, or better, establishing a link between the two worlds.

Right away, I realize, we have trouble understanding this, for we are very conditioned by two classical views of "heaven" and "earth." The first comes from the ancient philosopher Epicurus, who said that the realm of the gods has nothing to do with this world, which is marked by randomness and purposelessness. It is just a world made up of atoms that bump into each other by chance, and this world, accordingly, has no meaning. How like this is to modern forms of scientism and materialism! The other ancient view, still popular today, is that of Plato. Plato held that this world is a lesser realm and that the purpose of life is to get away from it as quickly as we can and make it to the higher realm of pure spirit. Life in these bodies is like life in a prison, and breaking free of the prison is the whole point.

Then there is the biblical view. For the Bible, heaven and earth are meant to come together. God, after all, created the material world and everything in it. He designed human beings to be his special representatives within that world, to offer praise on behalf of all of material creation and to reflect God's goodness to the rest of creation. Sin indeed led to a rupture between heaven and earth, but God launched a great rescue operation designed to bring the two worlds together.

Accordingly, he sent all sorts of messengers, including spiritual ones. But his rescue operation came to its full expression when he sent his Son to be the true King, to bring this world back on line with God's purposes. Isn't it wonderful that Jesus' central message is that of a kingdom and that his great prayer includes the line "thy kingdom come, thy will be done, on earth as it is in heaven"? That is a beautiful expression of this coming together of heaven and earth.

Now listen precisely to what the angel who appeared in the hills around Bethlehem says. First, the angel declares, "Do not be afraid." How that phrase echoes up and down the Scriptures!

When a being from a higher dimension breaks into our world, he typically says, "Fear not." Paul Tillich, the great Protestant theologian, commented that fear is the fundamental human problem, that fear undergirds most forms of human dysfunction. Because we are afraid, we crouch protectively around ourselves; because we are afraid, we lash out at each other in violence. If Christmas means that God is with us, that God is one of us, that God has come close, then we do not have to be afraid. How wonderfully Pope St. John Paul II picked up on this theme: "Be not afraid!"

The angel goes on: "For behold, I proclaim to you good news of great joy that will be for all the people." Good news, or *euangelion*—the Gospel (or God spell). The angel of Bethlehem is the first great evangelist, for he tells the Good News, which is meant for all people; this is why Jesus will tell his disciples to declare his lordship to the ends of the earth. What precisely is the Good News? "For today in the city of David a savior has been born for you who is Christ and Lord." Savior is *Soter* in Greek, which means "healer." This was rendered in Latin as *Salvator.* Can you see how our word "salve" is derived from the same source? It is a commonplace of myth and legend that the true king would bring healing to his country, just as a wicked king makes the whole country sick.

Further, this healer is "Christ and Lord." *Christos* just means anointed, for David had been anointed king by the prophet Samuel, and all of his successors had been anointed. This baby will be the point of ordering for all the world, the ruler and governor who sets the tone. And this is further emphasized by calling him "Lord"—*Kyrios* in Greek, *Dominus* in Latin. He is the one who should dominate us, who should rule over every aspect of our lives. After announcing the Good News of the birth of Christ, there appears a heavenly "host," or *stratia*, which is the Greek word for army. Do not get sentimental about these angels; they represent the army of heaven, which is more powerful than all of the armies of earth.

The first Christmas homily ever given was spoken on the Judean hills surrounding the little town of Bethlehem. And it begins with the proclamation of a heavenly messenger from above: Do not be afraid! Christ—the Savior, the Lord, the King of all the earth—is born!

THE CHRISTMAS SEASON

"The child grew and became strong, filled with wisdom; and the favor of God was upon him."

—LUKE 2:40

THE "LITTLE CHURCH" OF THE FAMILY

1 Samuel 1:20–22, 24–28 (Feast of the Holy Family, Year C)

In those days Hannah conceived, and at the end of her term bore a son whom she called Samuel, since she had asked the LORD for him. The next time her husband Elkanah was going up with the rest of his household to offer the customary sacrifice to the LORD and to fulfill his vows, Hannah did not go, explaining to her husband, "Once the child is weaned, I will take him to appear before the LORD and to remain there forever; I will offer him as a perpetual nazirite."

Once Samuel was weaned, Hannah brought him up with her, along with a three-year-old bull, an ephah of flour, and a skin of wine, and presented him at the temple of the LORD in Shiloh. After the boy's father had sacrificed the young bull, Hannah, his mother, approached Eli and said: "Pardon, my lord! As you live, my lord, I am the woman who stood near you here, praying to the LORD. I prayed for this child, and the LORD granted my request. Now I, in turn, give him to the LORD; as long as he lives, he shall be dedicated to the LORD." Hannah left Samuel there.

There are, to be sure, family values on display in the Bible, but they are probably not the ones we would naturally expect. We might in fact be taken aback when we see just how harsh, blunt, and demanding most biblical accounts of family relations are. We tend to be rather sentimental when it comes to families (especially this time of year), and there is nothing wrong with warm family feelings. But the scriptural attitude toward families isn't sentimental; it's theological and mission-focused.

A prime example of this unique biblical perspective is a passage from the beginning of 1 Samuel. We hear of Hannah, a devout Israelite woman who, to her deep chagrin and embarrassment, was not able to bear children. Every year, she went to the temple at Shiloh to pray for the grace of pregnancy. Once, she was praying with such passion and with so many tears that Eli the priest assumed that she was drunk and making a shameful display.

Displaying less than exemplary pastoral sensitivity, he said, "How long will you make a drunken show of yourself? Sober up from your wine!" Can you imagine a more miserable scenario for Hannah? But she stood her ground, protesting, "It isn't that, my lord. . . . I am an unhappy woman. I have had neither wine nor liquor; I was only pouring out my troubles to the LORD." Then she told Eli precisely how she had been entreating the Lord: "O LORD of hosts, if you look with pity on the misery of your handmaid . . . if you give your handmaid a male child, I will give him to the LORD for as long as he lives" (1 Sam. 1:9–19). Hannah promised to give her son as a nazarite, an ancient Israelite version of a monk, a person who was completely dedicated to God. This is an extraordinary prayer: Lord, please give me a child, and in gratitude, I will give the child back to you.

We then hear that the Lord heard Hannah's prayer, and in due time, she conceived and bore a son, whom she named Samuel, which means "asked of the Lord." When the child was weaned, his mother fulfilled her vow and brought him to the temple. She gave Samuel to Eli and told the priest to raise the child in the temple as a man of God. We can only begin to conceive the anguish Hannah must have felt as she offered back to Yahweh the child whom she had begged from the Lord with such intensity. In time, of course, Samuel grew to be one of the most powerful and important prophets in Israel, the one who anointed both Saul and David and set thereby the history of salvation in a decisively new direction.

With that story in mind, we can compare it to the well-known Gospel account of the finding of the child Jesus in the temple. After their visit to Jerusalem, Mary and Joseph, along with a bevy of their family and friends, were heading home to Nazareth. They presumed that the child Jesus was somewhere among his relatives in this caravan. Instead, he was in the temple of the Lord, conversing with the elders and masters of the law. Distraught, Mary and Joseph spent three days looking for him.

Any parent who has ever searched for a lost child knows the anguish they must have felt. Can you imagine what it was like as they tried to sleep at night, spinning out the worst scenarios in their minds? When they finally find him, they, with understandable exasperation, upbraid him: "Son, why have you done this to us? Your father and I have been looking for you with great anxiety." But Jesus responds with a kind of devastating laconicism: "Why were you looking for me? Did you not know that I must be in my Father's house?" (Luke 2:48–49).

Both stories convey a truth that runs sharply counter to our sensibilities—namely, that even the most powerful familial emotions and sentiments must, in the end, give way to mission. Though they felt an enormous pull in the opposite direction, both Hannah and Mary let their sons go, allowing them to find their vocation in the temple—which is to say, in the space of God.

Legitimate sentiment devolves into sentimentality precisely when it comes to supersede the call of God. Both narratives disclose that, on a biblical reading, the family is, above all, the forum in which both parents and children are able to discern their missions. It is perfectly good, of course, if deep bonds and rich emotions are cultivated within the family, but those relationships and passions must cede to something that is more fundamental, more enduring, more spiritually focused. The paradox is this: precisely in the measure that everyone in the family focuses on God's call for one another, the family becomes more loving and peaceful.

This biblical prioritization of values helps us to see, in fact, what typically goes wrong with families. When something other than mission is dominant—a son's athletic achievement, a daughter's success at university, a child's emotional reliance on her parents, etc.—family relationships actually become strained. The father may be trying to work out his unfulfilled dreams through his son, which becomes the center of his preoccupations. All of his feelings, his passions, and his energies are focused now around the success of his son. Or the mother, out of pride, drives a daughter to perfection in all things, not for her good, but out of the mother's self-regard. Or to maintain a superficial sense of peace, the dysfunctional behavior of children is left unaddressed. Sometimes this works the other way around: the children use their parents as a source of money or emotional security.

The point is that, ultimately, the family is the forum for the discovery and cultivation of one's mission from God. John Paul II admirably summed up what I've been driving at when he spoke of the family as an "ecclesiola" (a little church). At its best, he implies, the family is a place where God is worshiped and where the discernment of God's mission is of paramount importance. I know it seems strange to say, but the most loving thing that family members can do is to let each other go—for God's service.

HASTE, AMAZEMENT, AND REFLECTION

Luke 2:16–21 (Solemnity of Mary, the Holy Mother of God; Octave Day of Nativity)

The shepherds went in haste to Bethlehem and found Mary and Joseph, and the infant lying in the manger. When they saw this, they made known the message that had been told them about this child. All who heard it were amazed by what had been told them by the shepherds. And Mary kept all these things, reflecting on them in her heart. Then the shepherds returned, glorifying and praising God for all they had heard and seen, just as it had been told to them.

When eight days were completed for his circumcision, he was named Jesus, the name given him by the angel before he was conceived in the womb.

There are three words that I love from this brief passage from Luke's Gospel: "haste," "amazed," and "reflected." Each says something important about the spiritual life.

Luke tells us that "the shepherds went in haste to Bethlehem and found Mary and Joseph, and the infant lying in the manger."

Heavenly visitors had told them to do something, and they did it, and this is to their infinite credit. Similarly, after Mary accepted the angel's invitation at the Annunciation, she went "in haste" to visit her cousin Elizabeth (Luke 1:39). Once you hear the word of God, once heaven opens up to you, it is time to act.

The Bible is a book of mission. No figure in the Scripture ever communes with God without being sent to do something. Abraham, Jacob, Moses, Isaiah, Jeremiah, Peter, Paul, and all the rest are told that God has a task for them. Each and every baptized person has a definite task, and once you know what that is, you should not dawdle, procrastinate, or make excuses; you should go in haste. One of the central tragedies of the spiritual life is that we know what God wants us to do, and we don't do it. Be like the shepherds; be about the work that the Lord has given you to do!

John Henry Newman said, "God has created me to do some definite service; he has committed some work to me which he has not committed to another. I have my mission." God, in his infinite wisdom, has brought us into being; this is not a meaningless event. Our very existence is the result of God's intention. God wants to accomplish something through us. This is called vocation, and there is nothing more important in life than the determination of this vocation. Once we know it, we must go, move, act—in haste.

The second word I would like to consider is "amazed." Our reading says that all who heard the shepherds' story were amazed by it. It is true that God is found in ordinary things and places and events. All things, in some way, speak of God, and it is good not to be looking at every moment for amazing manifestations. However, we have not just a natural religion, not just a human spirituality, but a revealed religion. This means that the essential matters are not contained so much in the ordinary events and things of the world; they are communicated through extraordinary people and happenings. At the very heart of revelation are certain extraordinary things that God has done. God chose Abraham, and from that choice flows the whole history of Israel. God chose Moses and sent him on the definite mission to liberate his people. God brought the Israelites miraculously out of Egypt. God summoned the prophets—Isaiah, Jeremiah, Ezekiel, and the rest. God has acted decisively in history, breaking into the ordinary run of events, revealing his will and purpose to us. Nowhere is this truer than in the central claim of the Christian faith that God has become a little child, that God has become one of us. The Lord of creation, the infinite ground of being, the transcendent and self-sufficient God, has become a baby. That is (and there really is no other word) amazing. If the central truth of the Christian faith has been domesticated to the point that we are no longer knocked for a loop by it, something has gone decisively wrong. If we are not amazed by the baby of Bethlehem, we are not really paying attention.

G.K. Chesterton, reflecting on the Church's depictions of

the saints, noted that their open eyes "are frightfully alive . . . staring with a frantic intentness outward." This is the amazement that seizes every Christian. We, like the shepherds, are called to have our eyes wide open in wonder at what God has done. This, by the way, is what makes evangelization possible—this supernaturally oriented surprise. In fact, isn't communicating their amazement to others what evangelists do?

Finally, I would like to emphasize a word associated with Mary, the Mother of God: reflection. "Mary kept all these things, reflecting on them in her heart." Mary certainly went in haste; she knew her mission and she did it. And Mary was, undoubtedly, amazed by all the things that happened to her and her child. But she took a third step: in the quiet of her heart and mind, she treasured these things. She pondered them, turned them over, sought out their causes, saw their implications, and allowed them to work their way into the marrow of her bones.

Someone who really loves Shakespeare will watch and read *Hamlet* over and over. The play is simply inexhaustible; as the reader moves through life, her understanding of it changes and deepens as she allows it to wash over her. Someone who really loves Beethoven will have a similar relationship to the Ninth Symphony. No matter how many times he hears it, he always takes something new from it. And someone who really loves baseball will likewise learn how to treasure each game.

How much more is this the case in regard to the deepest, richest, most beautiful thing of all? Mary reflects upon the astonishing fact that God, through her fiat, has become one of us. Here, she becomes the model for all of us. We must pray over, contemplate, and meditate on the great events of Christmas. We must allow these things to move deeply into our hearts. St. John Henry Newman said that this treasuring quality of Mary makes her the patroness of theology. He furthermore observed that theology is one of the marks of a healthy Catholicism. Augustine, Aquinas, Bonaventure, Dante, Teresa of Avila, John of the Cross, John Paul II, and Newman himself are all Marian figures in this sense.

So be hasty when you know your mission, be amazed by what God has done, and never stop reflecting on these things in your heart.

WE OBSERVED HIS STAR AT ITS RISING

Matthew 2:1–12 (Solemnity of the Epiphany)

When Jesus was born in Bethlehem of Judea, in the days of King Herod, behold, magi from the east arrived in Jerusalem, saying, "Where is the newborn king of the Jews? We saw his star at its rising and have come to do him homage." When King Herod heard this, he was greatly troubled, and all Jerusalem with him. Assembling all the chief priests and the scribes of the people, he inquired of them where the Christ was to be born. They said to him, "In Bethlehem of Judea, for thus it has been written through the prophet:

And you, Bethlehem, land of Judah,
are by no means least among the rulers of Judah;
since from you shall come a ruler,
who is to shepherd my people Israel."

Then Herod called the magi secretly and ascertained from them the time of the star's appearance. He sent them to Bethlehem and said, "Go and search diligently for the child. When you have found him, bring me word, that I too may go and do him homage." After their audience with the king they set

> out. And behold, the star that they had seen at its rising preceded them, until it came and stopped over the place where the child was. They were overjoyed at seeing the star, and on entering the house they saw the child with Mary his mother. They prostrated themselves and did him homage. Then they opened their treasures and offered him gifts of gold, frankincense, and myrrh. And having been warned in a dream not to return to Herod, they departed for their country by another way.

Why does this story of the Epiphany so haunt us? Why have poets and artists and painters over the centuries returned to its themes again and again? It is, to be sure, a great story, full of drama and pathos, life and death, startling paradox and fascinating characters. But there is more to it than that. This tale also contains some elemental theological themes close to the heart of Christian revelation.

One of them has to do with the relationship between Christianity and the nations. We hear something extraordinary: Magi from the East—presumably from Babylon, where there was a well-developed culture of star-gazing—left their home country in search of a newborn king, whose star they had observed at its rising. Now, stop and think for a moment: Why, precisely, would people leave their own country in order to worship a foreign king at his birth? Perhaps we could imagine a loyal Israelite journeying to see his own king, or a loyal Babylonian coming to visit a newborn Babylonian king. But why would a Babylonian be excited at the birth of an Israelite ruler? This would be somewhat like an American going out of his way to reverence a new king in Europe. Wouldn't we find that just a little odd?

Love of one's own country and culture is one of the most basic passions in the human heart, and this passion has given rise both to beautiful expressions of patriotism and to some of the most egregious expressions of brutality in human history. Just look at the biblical history: the constant war of nation against nation, culture against culture, people against people. Of course, the same thing can be seen in the history of any nation from any part of the world. Egypt maintained itself through domination of its enemies, as did Assyria, Babylon, Greece, Rome, England, France—and, frankly, so does America to this day. Look at any of the trouble spots in the world today and you find the same thing: the war of nation-states, the war of cultures and peoples. This odd story, which comes close to the heart of the biblical revelation, should get our attention right away: Magi seek out a foreign king who somehow, nevertheless, belongs to them.

Of all the nations of the world, God chose Israel to be especially his own, a priestly people, a holy nation. But the reason for this choice was not to glorify Israel over and against the other nations; rather, it was to make of Israel a beacon to the world, so that through Israel all might be gathered. Yes, a king would be born for the Jews, but he would not be for the Jews alone; this Messiah would be the King of kings, a light to all the nations. We can hear this in the beautiful prophecies of Isaiah: Mount Zion, the true pole of the earth; there, all the tribes go up, all the nations united around Israel. That was the mission and the purpose and the vocation of Israel. The Messiah, therefore, would represent the overcoming of the nations, the transcending of the disputes between peoples and cultures that had so tragically marked human history. Do the Magi, in an inchoate way, sense this? When they are visiting this newborn king of Israel, they are not simply visiting a local potentate but the King of all the nations.

How wonderful that the sign of the birth of this King should be a star, something that can be clearly seen by every nation and draw like a magnet any and all peoples. A star belongs to no one in particular, precisely because it transcends any and all divisions here below. When the Magi saw it, they were willing to leave their own country behind—not because they hated their own nation, but because they had found something greater than it. In this newborn king, something had appeared that would relativize the ultimacy of any and all nations.

Once they had worshiped him, they went back to their own country "by another way." As Fulton Sheen pointed out, "No one who ever meets Christ with a good will returns the same way as he came." You can leave your country as a tourist and come back the same way; you can leave your country as a soldier and come back the same way; but these Magi left their country and came back "by another way." They were changed; they would remain Babylonians, but they had found a king who made them citizens of a higher country.

There is a strange and wonderful echo of this story in the account of the Crucifixion: raised up on Mt. Calvary, Jesus' cross bears a sign that reads, "Jesus of Nazareth, King of the Jews." But the sign is written in Hebrew, Latin, and Greek—that is to say, to all the nations. The crucified Lord is the love that transcends all the violence and disputatiousness of the nations. This is why Paul can say, "There is neither Jew nor Greek, there is neither slave nor free person, there is not male and female; for you are all one in Christ Jesus" (Gal. 3:28).

Do you realize that you belong, according to your deepest identity, to a Mystical Body that stretches across space and time? You are not primarily an American or a Frenchman or a Spaniard. You are, first and foremost, a member of an international and transnational organism. The Catholic Church is not a collectivity of likeminded people; it is not a club or an organization. The Church is an organism, a living body made up of cells and molecules and interdependent organs. When you are a Catholic, you can be at home in any nation, because your identity as a Catholic transcends any national identity. Part of the genius of Pope St. John Paul II was to make this concretely and viscerally real at World Youth Day. In Manila, Paris, Denver, Rome, and other sites all over the world, he allowed young people to see their connection through Christ to people of myriad races, languages, cultures, and nations.

How wonderful and odd that all of you reading this right now—regardless of your national or racial or cultural loyalties—come together in worshiping the King of the Jews!

PRIEST, PROPHET, AND KING

Acts 10:34–38 (Baptism of the Lord)

Peter proceeded to speak to those gathered in the house of Cornelius, saying: "In truth, I see that God shows no partiality. Rather, in every nation whoever fears him and acts uprightly is acceptable to him. You know the word that he sent to the Israelites as he proclaimed peace through Jesus Christ, who is Lord of all, what has happened all over Judea, beginning in Galilee after the baptism that John preached, how God anointed Jesus of Nazareth with the Holy Spirit and power. He went about doing good and healing all those oppressed by the devil, for God was with him."

In the Acts of the Apostles, Peter recounts how the baptism of Jesus by John marked the beginning of his public ministry. This feast provides us an opportunity to reflect on the meaning of our own Baptism and what it means for us as Christians. It has been said, truly enough, that the most important day of your life was the day of your Baptism, the day when you were grafted onto Christ, conformed to Jesus who is priest, prophet, and king. I would like to spend a little time with each of those categories.

Every baptized person is a priest. A priest is someone who prays, intercedes, and performs sacrifices. Old Testament priests include Adam, Noah, Abraham, Jacob, Ezekiel, and Moses. For centuries, Jewish priests performed sacrifices in the great temple of Jerusalem. And of course, Jesus is the high priest. Priests are border-walkers, mediators, friends of God. You might be thinking, "I'm not a priest; I'm not ordained." Yes, but you were chrismated, anointed, as a priest, which means that you must be a person of prayer—and I mean here intercessory prayer, prayer on behalf of the people of God. It has pleased God to channel his providential care precisely through us and through the instrumentality of our prayer.

Parents, do you pray regularly for your children? Children, do you pray for your parents, teachers, and coaches? Husbands, do you pray for your wives—and wives for your husbands? Do you pray before meals—both privately and publicly? Parents, do you bless your children before they go to bed and as they head off to school?

And do you attend Mass? The premier place where our common baptismal priesthood is acted out is the liturgy. Vatican II famously called for the "fully conscious and active participation" of the laity at Mass. By your participation, you enter into communion with Christ and join yourself to his sacrifice. One of the tragedies of the postconciliar period is that so many Catholics, by staying away from Mass, are abdicating this fundamental responsibility, turning from this incomparable privilege.

Next, as a baptized person, you are a prophet. A prophet is someone who speaks for God. Old Testament prophets include Moses, Isaiah, Jeremiah, Daniel, Hosea, Amos, Zechariah, and Elijah. Their task was to speak God's word in season and out, when that word was popular and when it was not—and, on the biblical telling, it most often was not. Jeremiah ends up thrown into a cistern and then put to death; Daniel is tossed into a lion's den; Elijah is pursued by the army of Jezebel. The prophet of prophets, of course, is Jesus himself, who is called the very Word of God.

If you are baptized, you have been anointed to preach. This means that the words of God should be on your lips regularly. You should speak of God and of the centrality of God to your life. You should wear signs of the faith on your person and display them at your place of work. You should preach with the beauty of your life, so that people might understand Christ through you. You ought to become a reader of theology and spirituality so that you might be able "to give an explanation to anyone who asks you for a reason for your hope" (1 Pet. 3:15). You must know that we inhabit a society that is increasingly hostile to religion in general and to Christianity in particular. Can you answer its questions with confidence and love?

Parents, do you actively teach the faith to your kids? At their Baptism, you promised to be their first teachers in the faith. Do they know how to pray? Do they understand the importance of the Mass? Do they know the saints and the doctrines of the

Church? Do they know what is going on during the liturgy? If not, you have not been preaching.

Finally, every baptized person is anointed as a king. A king, in the biblical sense, is someone who leads others to God, someone who orders things so that people find their mission. Great Old Testament kings include Moses, David, Solomon, Josiah, and Hezekiah. And of course, Jesus is the King of kings. Grafted onto him, you by your Baptism became a king. You might be thinking, "I'm not a pastor or a bishop; how could I fulfill the function of kingship in the Church?" Whenever you give someone good counsel in the spiritual life, when you direct them to the end that God wants them to achieve, you are acting as a king.

Whenever a mother or father takes control of their family so as to assure that everyone therein is growing in holiness, he or she is acting as a king. When you help your children to find their particular mission in life, you are playing a kingly role. When you take on leadership of any kind within the parish—parish council, finance council, education, fundraising, communications—you are acting as a king. When you help to organize a prayer group or a group to protest at an abortion clinic, you are acting as a king.

We never simply watch the baptism of Jesus from the outside as surveyors of a distant historical scene. We participate in it now, as priests, prophets, and kings!